Praise for
THE FRONTLINE CEO
and Eric Strafel

"What would happen if everyone had a chance to lead, not just those at the very top of the hierarchy? Eric Strafel answers this provocative question in *The Frontline CEO* and shows us how to unleash our collective talent on the problems that matter most. It's essential reading for anyone who's not satisfied with the status quo."

—FRANCES X. FREI, Professor of Technology and Operations Management at Harvard Business School, and **ANNE MORRISS,** Executive Founder of The Leadership Consortium, authors of *Unleashed: The Unapologetic Leader's Guide to Empowering Everyone Around You*

"Your company can't disrupt unless your people do. But they can't and won't if you don't. In this book, veteran CEO Eric Strafel takes you to the front lines and shows you how."

—WHITNEY JOHNSON, CEO of Disruption Advisors and author of *Build an A-Team* and *Disrupt Yourself*

"An outstanding framework for leaders in all fields, *The Frontline CEO* provides insight and incitement with winning lessons from the leading edge of business and life. Both practical and purposeful, this is a book for our times filled with lessons for the future. Read it."

—JAMES KERR, bestselling author of *Legacy: 15 Lessons in Leadership*

"The right book at the right time! Eric Strafel's strategies help you activate the core power source in any business—the frontline worker. Drawing on his real-world executive leadership experience and his insights into the needs of today's workers, he offers practical actions for business owners. Apply them to create a triple win for you, your employees, and your customers!"

—**LEE J. COLAN,** PhD, advisor to CEOs and author of
Engaging the Hearts and Minds of All Your Employees

"At a time when so many feel disillusioned with traditional workplaces, Eric Strafel shares a leadership model that is both inclusive and innovative. *The Frontline CEO* is the new guide to ensure your organization attracts, retains, and develops the very best talent in the ecosystem."

—**PAMELA SLIM,** author of *Body of Work*
and *The Widest Net*

THE
FRONTLINE
CEO

TURN EMPLOYEES INTO DECISION MAKERS
WHO INNOVATE SOLUTIONS,
WIN CUSTOMERS, AND BOOST PROFITS

ERIC STRAFEL

New York   Chicago   San Francisco   Athens   London   Madrid
Mexico City   Milan   New Delhi   Singapore   Sydney   Toronto

1 2 3 4 5 6 7 8 9   LCR   26 25 24 23 22 21

ISBN   978-1-264-25780-5
MHID   1-264-25780-5

e-ISBN   978-1-264-25781-2
e-MHID   1-264-25781-3

Library of Congress Cataloging-in-Publication Data

Names: Strafel, Eric, author.
Title: The frontline CEO : turn employees into decision makers who innovate
    solutions, win customers, and boost profits / Eric Strafel.
Description: New York : McGraw Hill, [2022] | Includes bibliographical
    references and index.
Identifiers: LCCN 2021013240 (print) | LCCN 2021013241 (ebook) |
    ISBN 9781264257805 (hardback) | ISBN 9781264257812 (ebook)
Subjects: LCSH: Personnel management. | Customer relations | Leadership.
Classification: LCC HF5549 .S8818 2022 (print) | LCC HF5549 (ebook) |
    DDC 658.3—dc23
LC record available at https://lccn.loc.gov/2021013240
LC ebook record available at https://lccn.loc.gov/2021013241

McGraw Hill books are available at special quantity discounts to use as premiums and sales promotions or for use in corporate training programs. To contact a representative, please visit the Contact Us pages at www.mhprofessional.com.

To Koen, Grayson, and Elin—
the inspiration behind my purpose

CONTENTS

ACKNOWLEDGMENTS

I am forever grateful for all the help and support of family and friends, colleagues and mentors, coaches, editors, and all the other people who supported me in finishing this book. It was a three-year-long journey of learning and growth, highs and lows, and self-discovery.

A huge thanks to my wife, Shelby, who supported me while working late nights, early mornings, weekends, and vacations to develop the ideas and stories in this book. She and our three kids, Koen, Grayson, and Elin, kept me grounded, gave me space when I needed it, and a loving hug when I needed it more. I look forward to spending extra time on family vacations in the future to repay my debt to them.

The process of writing a book takes perseverance, and my book coach, Robin Colucci, and collaborator, Dylan Hoffman, were with me every step of the way. Big thanks to my agent, Linda Konner, and my editor at McGraw Hill, Casey Ebro, who were great partners in helping me navigate the publishing process. As a first-time author, the guidance and insights each one of you provided were invaluable. Thank you all for making this a reality.

I am blessed to have a network of very intelligent, thought-provoking friends who helped me hone the book's key concepts. They are an elite group of thought leaders, visionaries, mentors—driven to be all they can be while staying balanced—and they all spurred me on to do the same. Mike Covert, Steve Dumaine, Joshua Sepkowitz, Barry Hill, and Zach Parham, I can't thank you enough for the monthly support and encouragement through the entire three-year journey! Judson Garrett, your depth of knowledge in the history of leadership is unparalleled, and I thank you for working with me to evolve my messaging with a nod to the past. One more big thank you goes out to Aaron Conner, a close friend and fellow martial arts enthusiast who sat with me on Thanksgiving 2017 and told me I needed to write a book. That conversation kicked this whole thing off. Aaron, it's DONE!

A heartfelt thank you to my parents and siblings, grandparents, cousins, aunts, and uncles, all of whom helped instill the values that made me who I am today, and whose influence continues to help me become a better person year after year. I hope this book makes you proud. Finally, these acknowledgments would be woefully incomplete if I failed to mention Ron Utke, my former boss turned avid supporter at Honeywell. Though he is no longer with us, I will never forget how he demonstrated an unwavering belief in me before I believed in myself. Saying thank you will never be enough, Ron. Your logical perspective is ever present in my approach to breaking down complex concepts so everyone can participate in developing solutions. You are the sherpa in my head.

FOREWORD

In a world where the contours of the economy are moving increasingly toward a way of life that recognizes the value of knowledge-intensive activities, *The Frontline CEO* has a timely, relevant, and important message for those who aspire to fill leadership positions in the boardroom and C-Suites, lead company town hall meetings, manage shop floors, or are otherwise engaged in lifelong learning.

Eric Strafel examines organizational design and alignment in a disruptive environment and rightfully concludes that businesses in the knowledge economy will thrive or fail based on their ability to unlock ideas, information, and best practices from a highly skilled workforce. His work brings years of leadership, management, and personal coaching that is framed and shared in the form of sage experience, analytic insight, and corporate success—measured not only by top-line/bottom-line growth but by an organizational climate that unlocks the innovative promise of the workforce community for the benefit of the reader.

Succinctly put, *The Frontline CEO* provides a critical look into the formula for future business success: build an organization and team that can grow together. In doing so, Eric Strafel helps us understand the key to accessing the intellectual wealth of the company—not in terms of contracts between the employee and the firm but with the covenant relationship among members of the team.

—Admiral Patrick M. Walsh, USN (Ret)
Cofounder of The First Watch Group

INTRODUCTION

The seeds of this book were planted in early 2016 when I became the CEO of Aviall, which at the time was a nonintegrated subsidiary of Boeing. It was my first experience in the role of CEO, and it gave me an opportunity to put a theory I had about leadership into action: growth and change come from clarifying a shared vision, and then prioritizing the empowerment of people at all levels to achieve that vision. Leadership, more than anything, is about helping others be their best. So I asked a lot of questions. I asked the employees how they felt about the company, how well they understood and connected to Aviall's purpose, and how they thought we could operate in alignment with that purpose and deliver improved results. Through this process, together, we developed a new strategy oriented toward our higher purpose, with an eye toward fostering inclusion in our ranks.

After that, I made available every resource I could and tried to create space for others to lead by staying out of their way. To my great joy (though hardly to my surprise), they achieved remarkable results. Through the efforts and commitment of all our teams, Aviall won awards from GI Jobs and the National Guard for our support of veterans, and from Cigna for the health and wellness of our employees. And because of the work our affinity groups did in the community, we were recognized by the United Way for our commitment to diversity and inclusion. We did this all while increasing the revenues and earnings of a $3 billion company by at least 20 percent every year for three years straight.

Eventually, Boeing elected to integrate Aviall and rebrand it as Boeing Distribution (though, for clarity, in this book, I will continue to refer to the company at this time as Aviall). I helped to lead that rebranding effort, and at the end of it, I moved into a leadership position within a $15 billion supply chain. My new position had its own challenges and opportunities, but given my journey so far—from a small two-year school in upstate New York to the CEO of a multibillion-dollar company—I felt I had something to share. I believed that perhaps, if I told my story, I could inspire other leaders to pursue a new version of leadership, one centered on service, humility, and a commitment to helping others.

I've spent many hours reflecting on why Aviall and its employees thrived during that period. I narrowed it down to a few representative moments: the time that our third-shift warehouse workers came up with our new company purpose; the consistent and enthusiastic engagement we received from more than 200 managers, each of whom understood our goals and found creative ways to make their jobs their own; and, more than anything else, all those open conversations with employees at every level I had the privilege to engage in as I'd walk the floor—including the many times that someone told me I was getting it wrong and how I could make it right. I started journaling about these experiences, and eventually my entries formed the foundation of this book.

As I wrote, I realized that diversity and inclusion kept cropping up in my thinking and writing. This made sense— although I'd been pondering questions about inclusion in the corporate world for a long time, my thoughts gained clarity and momentum in 2018. That year, I led a roundtable with a group of new leaders—all diverse, passionate, and highly capable—who expressed deep disillusionment with what they saw in business leaders around the world. They didn't think that successful leaders shared their values. They felt that most only worked to satisfy the quarterly demands of Wall Street when they should be serving their communities. Several even indicated that if all business leadership meant was boosting shareholder value, then maybe they didn't want to pursue a career in a traditional setting.

This worried me. Here was an entire generation of principled, intelligent, and caring business leaders who felt excluded. I could understand why. Most big organizations—including Fortune 500 companies and even government organizations—lacked the proper infrastructure to listen to their employees. Even companies that want to understand their employees' perspectives still used antiquated processes designed for a slow-moving, change-resistant world with limited communication capabilities. These old systems rely on top-down communication that systematically freezes out input from lower levels of the organization. These universally accepted norms privilege those already in positions of power while strangling diversity and inclusion. They also weaken the ability of a business to perform.

The only way to change this internal landscape is through concerted effort and initiative. With my background in engineering and systems analysis, I concluded that we needed to reengineer the mechanism of big organizations, replace the old top-down communication processes with two-way valves that allow for diverse interactions within a company, create space for listening, and encourage greater vision, inspiration, and innovation.

As part of my attempt to reengineer those mechanisms, I started a business coaching company, SUMMi7, that assists small and medium-sized businesses, especially those owned by women, people of color, and veterans, by leveraging our experience to help them scale with purpose. Our mission is to create a more equitable and diverse business ecosystem by providing support and resources to businesses owned by underserved and underrepresented groups. We focus on helping companies find their purpose, which we define as the reason a business exists beyond itself. Purpose naturally centers on customers, but there is often a higher purpose that creates a positive impact for society. We help these businesses scale with purpose and create meaningful impact for customers in a way that is both profitable and sustainable.

Not long after transitioning from the corporate world to the world of entrepreneurship, I began to scratch the surface in understanding the extent of the disadvantages that small and medium-sized businesses face; in particular, businesses owned by people of color and women. At Aviall, we had access to extensive leadership development programs, skills training, capital, and technology, as well as lots of other support. If I encountered a new problem or wanted advice on a specific initiative, I could call on numerous experts from a resource pool of more than 150,000 people in the company or hire consultants. Small and medium-sized businesses have none of that. So I asked myself, "How can I help make this a meritocracy? What can I do to fill some of the gaps for these companies, so that the people with the best ideas who put in the effort are *actually* the most successful?"

We've been working on that ever since. This book is part of that work. I hope it shows you—whether you're a young entrepreneur, manager, executive, or frontline worker experiencing the same frustrations of the group of disillusioned leaders I met with in 2018—that you can be successful without sacrificing your values.

I have always had a deep-rooted desire to contribute to a purpose: to know that the work I'm doing is clearly aligned with my company's vision and mission, as well as my own, and that I am making a meaningful contribution to our ability to serve customers and to drive company growth and profits while creating a positive impact in the lives of employees and the community. This is the higher purpose I refer to often throughout this book.

This higher purpose is then fueled when you can lead teams in which all employees are excited to go to work, to perform at their best because *they want to*, and they are unrestrained and empowered to do so. These inspired people know without a doubt and are able to see clearly that their work is essential to the company's overall success. They are shown daily how they are valued through support, inclusion, recognition, and compensation. When this higher purpose is met, I have seen time and time again, that businesses achieve new heights of performance and success beyond what was previously thought possible.

As a leader, you just have to remember one thing: It's not about you. It's about serving others.

There are three choices all leaders make, whether they realize it or not, that will determine the impact they will have, both in their industry and the world at large:

CHOICE #1: Is leadership about what you can achieve or what you can help others achieve in service of a greater purpose for your customers, community, and society?

I've worked for leaders who believed that their personal success trumped their employees' success. It's likely you have, too. At one point in my career, I was literally told to "stay in my lane" by a leader whose attitude restrained my development. During those years, it was frowned upon every time

I shared new ideas to improve our business, and my career was all but stalled. I've also worked for leaders who see the strengths of everyone on their teams, even when their backgrounds and experience are different from their own, and use those combined strengths not only to achieve more but also to improve every team member's performance.

CHOICE #2: Will you follow the path of others, or will you create a new path, building on the work of others that came before you, leveraging your unique strengths and shaped by your values?

Like many, I spent much of my early career trying to fit the predefined mold of other leaders. I tried to meet their expectations, and I worked hard to fit in. Although this can be a good starting point, it eventually will limit your growth as a person and as a leader. However, I also believe that self-imposed limitations are in our own heads, and a good leader can help you get out of that box, as others have done for me.

CHOICE #3: Will you battle to make your organization more inclusive, by simplifying complexity, being transparent with information, and creating access for everyone? Are you willing to do this even if, in the short term, it seems to put your own career trajectory at risk?

In my experience, employees commit the most to their work when management reduces the barriers to participation in leadership. When our management teams made information more accessible, simplified our processes, and gave people a chance to offer their own points of view, it always led to the best results. However, whenever we did this, it always felt like a risk. Removing complexity, improving transparency, encouraging and celebrating diversity—all of these acts shift the status quo. And to shift the status quo, especially in a way that promotes inclusion, requires you to break institutionalized processes and habits. This always makes me nervous, and, at first, it often felt like a slower, less efficient way of doing things. But it's not; it's just an adjustment. Usually, with faith and discipline, it leads to a more streamlined organization with highly effective teams. The end result is a business with unlimited potential and the ability to grow well beyond the previous status quo.

The leaders I've seen who respond to these challenges with complacency tend to stall, while the ones who take them on, successfully or not, continue to rise. As Theodore Roosevelt suggested in his famous "Citizen in a Republic" speech, the credit for great deeds belongs to those who try, even if they fail, and not to the critic who sits on the sidelines.

I invite you to read this book with an open mind, to be willing to question what you understand about authority and the role of a leader. I hope that by the time you finish it, you'll have gained a new perspective. I hope it will inspire you to double down on your commitment to set aside whatever ego and pursuit of glory you might have and engage in the hard work of self-reflection—to find out what you value and to move ahead in your own journey of discovery with the confidence to be yourself at all times.

The work is substantial, but the payoff is that you will find yourself in an organization that is not only absolutely killing it but one you are proud to lead.

LEAD FROM THE FRONT LINES

Since the first industrial revolution, large corporations have operated in a top-down leadership model, in which decision-making resides with the senior leaders and there's limited engagement and information exchange with the front-line employees who do the work. While that model led to many successes through the end of the twentieth century, it is too slow and bureaucratic to keep pace with change in the twenty-first century. Top-down companies fail to innovate fast enough and struggle to compete. Most go extinct or, at best, lose market share. In fact, of all the companies that were part of the Fortune 500 in 1955, by 2020 only 51, or just over 10 percent, remained.* This statistic hints at an important truth: top-down leadership lacks the agility that enables companies to compete and thrive in today's marketplace, and those that continue to operate in this way will succumb to the ever-shifting environment.

---

* Mark J. Perry, "Only 51 US companies have been on the Fortune 500 since 1955, thanks to the creative destruction that fuels economic prosperity," AEI, May 26, 2020, https://www.aei.org/carpe-diem/only-51-us-companies-have-been-on-the-fortune-500 -since-1955-thanks-to-the-creative-destruction-that-fuels-economic-prosperity/.

Not only is technology and the landscape of the global market changing faster than ever, the innovations of the late 2010s have accelerated the shift of customer expectations across multiple industries. Two of the most prominent examples of this are Uber and Amazon, both of which used technology to deliver unprecedented leaps in convenience and efficiency. Uber disrupted an entire industry by making a car available at your fingertips at any time, while Amazon enables you to shop on your device for almost anything you want and have it delivered even on the same day. As these revolutions in transportation and retail were realized, they suddenly altered customer expectations for every other industry. Organizations that fail to adapt quickly enough will continue to suffer.

Fortunately, you need look no further than your company's front lines to discover the key to its longevity. Ninety percent of employees in any given organization work on the front lines, and the few who don't usually started there. An organization's purpose is actualized on the front lines, and therefore it's vital that its leaders stay connected to what is happening there. The front lines are where we interact with customers, solve the most problems, establish norms, and cultivate culture. Put simply, an organization creates (and demonstrates) its value on its front lines. Thus, to remain competitive, organizations must embrace frontline leadership.

Frontline leadership is a system in which top-level executives break through traditional silos and engage with frontline employees to develop and implement strategies. With this approach, frontline workers are empowered to make decisions and iterate processes on their own. At its best, frontline leadership pulls employees into the decision-making process, so that solutions are sought, found, and acted upon in the area that matters most—where the work gets done. It strives to obtain diverse perspectives on a single issue and to break down barriers to participation by extending knowledge and authority to each employee. The end result is an environment that relies on the horizontal flow of information and ideas, one that fosters radical trust and inclusion.

Frontline leadership doesn't mean that employees and senior executives share the same responsibilities. A top-level leader's job is to provide the vision, to think ahead to what the company will look like 5, 10, and 15 years down the line. These leaders seek to understand the markets the company serves and the trends that will change those markets. They need to maintain a strategic plan for how to compete and win, and to share that information and their vision with employees in a way that empowers them to move in that direction. The frontline employee's primary job is to respond to what happens in the present—to adapt to changing customer needs and new expectations as they arise.

This leadership style can be difficult to imagine. It was for me, until I saw frontline leadership modeled successfully during my time as a procurement specialist at Honeywell. I had a chance to join our vice president of operations during a daily meeting with the supervisor and a few other employees from every manufacturing team on the site. We met in a huge room that could hold well over a hundred people. The room buzzed with energy as the VP welcomed everybody, and then asked them to report on how yesterday went, what needed to get done today, and what help they needed. Then he did something remarkable: he stopped talking. Each team took turns sharing their successes, needs, and struggles. When one team mentioned that it required support in a certain area, before the vice president could say anything, three or four other teams had jumped in to offer assistance. They collaborated across teams and across departments, combining their collective knowledge to develop richer solutions on the spot. The VP only spoke when he needed to—to give context about the state of the company, to allocate resources, or when a problem had no evident solution. For the most part, the teams ran the meeting.

This experience was transformative for me. Before that meeting, I thought that effective leadership required making the most decisions and being at the forefront of any effort to solve an issue. I used to measure my daily success by how many problems I'd attacked and how many decisions I'd made. This one meeting changed all that. I witnessed how frontline leadership was infinitely more powerful. It was obvious from the energy and engagement in that room, in the efficiency with which we resolved problems, in the joy the employees expressed as they worked together. It also bore out quantitatively, as that vice president oversaw a 40 percent improvement in supplier performance and a 20 percent improvement in output without adding resources. He did it simply by improving the utilization of labor and equipment and creating a culture in which people could attack any challenge they faced together.

As I've advanced in my career, I've seen the myriad of benefits that frontline leadership offers. Because top executives have intimate contact with and take guidance from the front lines, they have a much better sense of whether their decisions and initiatives are working and unfolding as planned, and they can course correct early if problems arise. And because employees have the freedom to work as autonomous, engaged, and driven individuals, they feel more respected and fulfilled in their jobs. That degree of satisfaction encourages people to contribute everything they can—all their discretionary effort, creative thinking, and unique ideas. All this dramatically improves efficiency and agility, which translates to higher profits and a greater market share.

Finally, and most vitally, because frontline employees have the clearest view of the customer at the point of delivery, a company that leads from the front lines always has the customer in sight. That means that each initiative and each investment can be crafted to respond to current customer needs, which improves return on investment and protects large corporations from losing market share to smaller, up-and-coming companies that might recognize a gap and fill it before the established company even knows it's there.

I've also worked in a top-down leadership model, and I've seen its shortcomings. Employees feel no ownership over new initiatives, so they don't buy in. Senior leaders waste the opportunity to shape culture and company values because they don't open up effective two-way communication with the front lines. The culture diverges. The executives might believe in quality and efficiency, but because they don't take the time to connect their workers to those values, the rest of the workforce operates based not on what is *expected* by the main office but on what is *accepted* at different sites.

The same lack of communication also means frontline workers don't have a deep enough understanding of new strategies to be able to implement them. This slows learning, and makes change and innovation nearly impossible. If you don't innovate, you will lose your competitive edge and your customers soon after.

There are two essential processes to establish a practice of frontline leadership. The first is that executives need to *lead from the front lines themselves*, meaning that they gather input and partner with their frontline workers to ensure that the solutions they develop together are effective. The second is to *create a climate where individual employees are empowered to become leaders in their own right*, with the knowledge, authority, and support to make their own decisions, iterate their own processes, and make course corrections on the fly. This much power residing in the front lines may trigger anxiety for some executives, with good reason. If done incorrectly, an empowered workforce can run in a hundred different directions, and pull the company out of alignment. That's partly why so few companies fully embrace this approach, even when they may believe in the benefits. That said, the risk of sacrificing agility by sticking to a top-down leadership strategy far outweighs the risk of embracing frontline leadership, especially when the company invests in the proper infrastructure to support frontline leaders. In fact, if you can successfully implement the ideas in this book, you will improve the quality of decision-making in your organization and gain speed, effectiveness, and buy-in among your workforce. The person best suited to solve a problem is the person who is closest to it. In most organizations, that is the person on the front lines. All they need are the tools and the support to do it.

These two processes—executives leading from the front lines and empowering frontline workers to become leaders—are interconnected. Progress in one leads to progress in the other. The transition from top-down to frontline leadership begins with upper levels of management recognizing the need to shift their leadership approach and then being willing to make the necessary changes—to be transparent with information, allow others to make decisions, and trust that the organization will move faster with a flatter distribution of authority.

Frontline leadership promotes inclusion and creates the conditions for others to lead, which fosters a long-term advantage for any organization. The primary factor that determines how well your company will make the shift to frontline leadership is how you show up as a leader. The first habit management must build is to lead by example. Go to the front lines to gather input from and collaborate with frontline employees. Once you master that, you can facilitate widespread frontline leadership by empowering each worker to become a leader.

Through my experience, I've identified five keys to help you make the transition to frontline leadership:

- Find your authentic leadership approach.
- Establish a dialogue with the front lines.
- See the whole person.
- Coach rather than direct.
- Roll up your sleeves and pitch in.

Find Your Authentic Leadership Style

I've spent a long time thinking about what inspires me, and I've come up with two answers: one, a leader who believes in his or her mission and purpose with such absolute conviction that I believe in it as well; and two, a leader who believes in me so much that I have no choice but to believe in myself. I've since strived to cultivate these two characteristics in how I lead. I advise any executive or manager who wants to shift to frontline leadership to think about what inspires you and to work to incorporate that into how you lead authentically.

Frontline leadership requires that you challenge employees to accomplish more than they thought possible and foster a shared belief that they can achieve it together. Higher-level leaders can spread that belief among frontline workers and create a ripple of positive energy that will spread throughout the entire organization, bringing people together. Inspiring employees on the front lines to lead will help people cultivate their own leadership practices and eventually grow to become strong leaders themselves.

However, before you can start to have that positive effect, before others believe in you, you must do the work to believe in yourself and develop your own authentic leadership style. You can do this by understanding your strengths, your values, and how you contribute most effectively to achieve the goals of your team or company. Inauthentic leaders—those who don't take the time to connect with people and aren't genuine and transparent in their intent—will struggle to inspire others. They might sugarcoat information about the company's status or an employee's performance. They may rely on canned feedback or platitudes, or even avoid giving feedback at all. An authentic leader can communicate to employees about where they stand and still show respect for them as individuals. An authentic leader knows how to provide guidance and support to help employees grow and move forward, and demonstrates that by listening and incorporating feedback. Authentic leadership relies on a robust, ongoing practice of self-awareness. It requires that you clarify your values as well as become aware of your strengths and weaknesses so you can position yourself to be your best while acknowledging you have your own challenges. Everyone is different, and everyone has something to contribute. By understanding how people work, you can strengthen relationships across teams and assure you're hiring people whose values are compatible with those of your organization.

I began to develop this awareness and explore my authentic values and leadership style in 2005. I started to keep the first couple of pages in my planner open as a space to reflect, record quotes that stuck with me, and keep track of key areas where I wanted to grow. To prompt my reflections, I would recall all of the times that I felt energized and excited about what was in front of me. By identifying the commonality in those moments, I recognized what kind of work and the type of work environment that really inspired me. This awareness was the start of my journey to understanding my own purpose and values.

Of course, values and purpose extend beyond the workplace into your personal life. Identifying these allows you to invest your free time in alignment with those values. Some good questions to ask to discover your values include: When given the freedom to choose, without any concern for other people's judgment, how do I choose to spend my time? What are the top five ways I would prioritize my time and energy? Is it with family? Pursuing personal development? Serving others? Contributing creatively?

In my personal reflections, a few core values kept cropping up: family, optimism, and hard work. It didn't take long to understand where these values came from. My value of family came from my parents, who lived that value their whole lives; my commitment to hard work was from my father, who was an electricianand was always there to help others; and my sense of optimism was from my mother, who always exuded confidence that we would figure out any problems, no matter how difficult they seemed.

As you grow in your career, other mentors and role models emerge, and many throughout my career have informed my values. I remembered how they embodied and led with their values, and how these were reflected in the ways that they conducted themselves. The qualities I saw in my mentors, including my parents, slowly shaped how I live my values in my everyday life. A constant struggle I had was to balance my career with my duties as a father and a husband. It's something I shared with my colleagues, since family was so important to me and it's the first challenge I began to openly share that started to get me comfortable being vulnerable as a leader. This helped to set a tone within any team I led that we would respect each other's commitments outside of work. I shared optimism by highlighting all of the amazing opportunities the future held in my communications with my teams, instead of fixating on the challenges that we faced. And I underscored the importance of hard work by always setting ambitious goals for my team that required everyone to work together, get out of their comfort zone, and try new things to acheive. The more challenging the goal, the greater the sense of accomplishment. Together, we discovered the joy of a job well done.

Growth is constant, and there's always a deeper level of self-knowledge to attain, so I still practice note-taking and self-reflection. It's provided something of a fossil record of my personal development, and it enables me to go back and see which experiences and thoughts have shaped my thinking. With this clarity, I can better articulate my values to my teams, continue to live in alignment with them, and lead in a way that's authentic. Beyond that, it provides a greater sense of empathy, as it's helped me recognize the accumulated experiences and struggles that go into shaping a person.

During my time at Aviall, one of the most successful approaches that helped others do this was to invite all team leaders to a series of workshops designed to help them discover their authentic leadership voice. We would always start out with an exercise in which they would identify two or three of their core values and then research a leader who demonstrates each. Everyone had to identify specific examples of how the leaders embodied those values, and then write down two or three concrete ways to express those values in how they lead. For example, one of my core values is serving others. In alignment with that, I prioritize mentoring team members.

This is one of many ways to help others develop personal awareness and lead more authentically. Experiment. Find a strategy that works best for you, whether it's my method, an adaptation of it, or something entirely different. What matters most is that you consistently reflect on and refine your values and get feedback from others you trust to see if you have any blind spots. Hold yourself accountable for living your values while recognizing nobody is perfect and we will all stumble, learn, and grow. And those challenges and how we recover are often what shape us most.

Establish a Dialogue with the Front Lines

For an organization to lead from the front lines, upper management and frontline teams must engage in a robust, ongoing dialogue and abandon the top-down communication style of executives passing down direction with little context or explanation. Dialogue operates like a rubber band wrapped around the executives and the frontline teams, binding both groups closer together. The ability for leaders to generate and nurture this bond with the front lines will pace an organizations ability to respond to the constantly changing environment in which we do business today.

To do so, start by cultivating two practices: listening and transparency. Executives and managers need to prioritize time in their day to listen actively to employees on the front lines and understand the challenges they face and what support they need. This broadens the perspective of the leadership team, giving executives access to deeper layers of knowledge and expertise that enable them to craft more dynamic, comprehensive solutions to the complicated problems of the twenty-first century. Transparency means that leaders at all levels communicate the honest, full truth about the financial health of the company, the markets the company competes in, and the rationale behind key decisions and actions. This transparency gives frontline leaders the information they need to make better decisions on the ground.

The way the vice president of operations at Honeywell led his meetings became a paragon of listening excellence for me. After taking over as CEO of Aviall, I wanted to replicate that same level of communication, engagement, and continuous improvement. To set the stage for increasing transparency, my leadership team and I hosted a quarterly all-employee meeting to discuss the state of the business, during which we encouraged everyone to highlight the successes and failures experienced in the quarter, to share the challenges they faced in their attempts to improve, to provide feedback on strategic initiatives, and to describe some real customer experiences. We also adopted the same kinds of weekly and daily team meetings I'd seen at Honeywell and had further developed over many years by that point, which became part of our natural operating rhythm.

But we wanted to go further, and we found a few great ways to do so. The first was a monthly meeting with all of our managers from around the world. Because of the time zone differences, we did each call twice, with 50 to 100 managers on each. For the first 30 minutes, I discussed the state of the company and shared the key decisions we'd made and actions we'd taken in the prior month, as well as the reasoning behind them. After that, I outlined our strategy for the next 30, 60, and 90 days, taking time to explain why we'd decided to follow the paths we chose. Finally, because all effective communication is a dialogue, I opened up the last 30 minutes to questions and input from the managers, so people from different teams could share and coordinate their efforts. I soon started inviting frontline leaders to join these meetings, and had them share the actions they'd taken, ways we'd found to better serve customers, and opportunities that had been identified for improvement.

We also published a weekly newsletter to highlight different teams around the company and how they contributed to our mission and purpose, and we held roundtable discussions at sites around the world to better understand the unique challenges of our global teams and incorporate their feedback.

We emphasized transparency in all of those initiatives at Aviall. We didn't just call meetings to give instructions or hear from employees, but also to share information and to answer the most important question: Why? *Why* are we, as a company, doing what we are doing? *Why* are certain decisions being made and actions taken at all levels of leadership? *Why* is your job important in serving our customers? When frontline employees understand the thinking behind a decision and the reason for a goal, then they can solve problems as they arise without the need for micromanaging from above. This is a key part of creating an inclusive organization in the age of knowledge workers. In traditional leadership models, siloed information serves as a major barrier that prevents frontline workers from participating in the daily course corrections needed to keep organizations performing at thier best.

In a transparent organization, employees know exactly what they're striving for and why, so they can draw upon their own knowledge to make informed decisions. Even better, frontline employees often work directly with customers, so they can easily extend their decision-making process beyond the confines of the company and consult with their customers directly. This increases agility, as it enables employees to respond to customer needs as they arise. Executives can monitor what happens on the front lines and see almost immediately the effectiveness of whatever changes are being made. With this information, an organization can iterate its broader strategies, and make course corrections in the middle of initiatives, which ultimately leads to better solutions for customers and shareholders. That's why I spent so much time in all of these meetings providing context and connecting everything we did back to the company's purpose—to empower our frontline workers through knowledge. To have frontline leadership, you must do the same. Many companies today have presented a vision for where the company is going, which is a great start. But you also have to connect with your purpose to reveal the why behind the moves you make.

See the Whole Person

To have an empowered workforce, you can't just focus on employees as workers. You have to uncover who they are as *people*. This requires you to create an environment in which everyone feels comfortable bringing his or her full, authentic selves to work. So much of the success of frontline leadership relies on employees putting in extra effort, approaching their jobs creatively, and being willing to rush in and fill any gaps that they see. There are two prima facie traits that all employees need before they will do that. The first trait, is the *desire* or motivation to expend that extra effort, and the second is the *energy* to execute. The fact is that being an empowered employee takes more effort. It requires more effort and the ability to feel comfortable with the vulnerability inherent in taking risks or innovating.

Being empowered makes work more meaningful for most people, even though they have to invest more of their time and energy. Yet if there's even a hint of bitterness or lack of trust in the workplace, then most employees won't make that investment.

The same worker can do the same job for two different companies with different cultures and produce opposite results. To thrive, employees need to be immersed in a culture that empowers them, in which they can leverage their strengths, learn through trial and error, and find the team camaraderie that reinforces their contributions. By creating an environment where people can be their best and find meaning in their work, you'll increase engagement and retention of employees who share your purpose and values.

When helping small businesses establish processes to manage employee performance, provide feedback, and develop their teams, I've used a few approaches to enable leaders to connect with their teams.

Make Sure All Employees Know How Their Jobs Support the Purpose of the Company

Your company's purpose is a description of the impact you want to make for customers—what you strive to achieve by solving a problem or providing value. Use every opportunity, from the first day a new employee walks in the door, to weekly or monthly one-on-ones, to all-team meetings, and so on, to keep the company's purpose front and center for your team, so employees can draw meaning from how they impact the world. Make sure every employee knows why customers choose you above your competitors, reinforcing that employee's work.

Understand the Aspirations of Your Employees

Discuss where they want to go with their careers, what they're passionate about, what's most important to them, and then help them move toward those goals. This could mean connecting them with a mentor who's aligned with their chosen career path, investing in training and development that supports their goals alongside the goals of your company, or providing opportunities to work on projects or external engagements that align with their passions outside of their normal job responsibilities. Not only do you recognize the whole person but you invest in the whole person, and thus develop leaders in your own ranks.

Integrate Work and Life

Create events that bridge the gap between work and people's lives outside of work. I experienced this as an engineer at Pratt & Whitney, my first job out of college. I moved from upstate New York to south Florida, where I didn't know anyone within 1,000 miles. Soon after I arrived, the company hosted a Family Day, and invited us to bring our families onsite to see the products we made. My parents visited Florida for the first time and saw the F-14 Tomcat and F-15 Eagle, two of the engines I'd worked on, which sat in the parking lot of our office building. It was one of the most impactful moments of my early career. I never imagined working on such amazing products and felt genuine pride in what I did. The cherry on top was that I was able to share that with my parents.

Many years later, with that experience in mind, we launched the Aviall Friends and Family Day in 2011. We invited employees and their families to tour our operations and see some of the aircraft we supported, with a Chinook, one of the largest rotorcraft, as the main draw. We got great feedback from our employees and continued to evolve the event to incorporate new activities. It allowed everyone to see different aspects of one another and to build connections beyond work.

Support Through Struggle

Like it or not, everyone will face huge challenges in their lives, and often, those challenges affect our work. Inclusive leaders will not only know when their teams are struggling with something difficult, they will help them through it. It's easy to achieve results when everything is perfect. A truly great leader helps employees through these challenges, and enables them to come back just as strong, or stronger, knowing that the company and its leaders are behind them. This might mean giving employees time off to grieve the passing of a loved one, connecting them with resources to support a specific need, or just providing them with the space to get through a difficult time. Because each challenge is unique, and each person reacts individually to it, there is no handbook for how to help your employees through tough times. But you'll never be able to if you haven't already established a relationship with open communication that allows people to talk about what's on their minds.

One approach to become better at noticing when employees are struggling, so you can help them through challenging times, is to practice mindfulness. Be present with team members by giving them your full, undivided attention, which will strengthen your ability to empathize with challenges they face. Empathy is one of the most beautiful, fundamental human connections you can make by experiencing what it's like to walk in someone else's shoes. But it's also one of the most difficult to experience in a high-pressure business environment—not because most leaders lack feeling, but because the day-to-day demands of business require so much attention, they prevent most people from slowing down enough to perceive the needs of others. This is compounded by the fact that many leaders feel a pressure to always be busy, taking on as many projects as possible. I fell into this trap early in my career, and it hindered my ability to remain present with my team members.

A leader who finds it difficult to slow down and focus on one person also stunts the ability of frontline employees to grow into leaders. One of my mentors said, "I try not to make any decisions that someone on my team can." That orientation alone represented mindfulness: my mentor had slowed down and thought through who on his team could best handle whatever came up. It also required him to provide support to his team members as they made their decisions. He had to stop and ask thoughtful questions to help employees work through problems. Doing this might seem hard at first, but not only does it lead to more intelligent decision-making, it accelerates the development of frontline employees and empowers your team in a way that multiplies success. Developing a practice of mindfulness—whether it's meditation, focusing on one activity at a time, or conscious breathing exercises—will enable you to be present with your employees and connect with them in a meaningful way.

The bottom line is that, as a manager, you have to take an authentic interest in your employees as people, get to know them, discover what they value, and understand what motivates them. Many managers and leaders lean toward the impersonal and construct an imaginary, yet unbreakable boundary. They talk to their employees only about work, which means they're acknowledging only a small part of what makes up that person. If you believe that people do their best work and are most engaged when they can be fully themselves, then you must acknowledge the other parts of their lives that make them who they are.

You can take this commitment to seeing the whole person further with your actions. My favorite way to do this is to acknowledge that people have other interests beyond work, and then do everything I can to ensure that they are able to pursue them. Although it may seem like doing so would lower productivity, I've found the opposite. When given the space to pursue what they enjoy away from work, people come to work with more energy to contribute. They don't dread the Monday morning alarm, watch the clock in the afternoon, or take sick days just to get a mental break.

When people can be themselves at work, leverage their strengths, and build true relationships with their coworkers, they get excited to see their teammates. People enjoy working with one another, knowing that they are contributing to something bigger, and sometimes lose track of time. I've felt this way at work many times, and even though it's not every day, it's more often than not. The benefits go the other direction as well. Having had a fulfilling day at work makes me a better father and husband because I leave feeling energized, not drained. I don't need time to decompress when I get home. I jump right into family time.

Once your employees experience joy and camaraderie at work, you can raise the bar and challenge them beyond what they thought they could achieve. They'll surprise even themselves. When a team is fully engaged and working together toward a common purpose, amazing things happen. My wife, a career Human Resources professional, has described my approach as setting a high expectation and then empowering people until it hurts. I think she's right. I believe that it's a leader's responsibility to bring out the best in people. Although it may be uncomfortable at times, the feeling of accomplishment for most when they have the autonomy to do their work their way and a leader who believes in them is one of the most rewarding things in life.

It doesn't take a lot of effort to help employees maintain balance in their lives. First, simply respect their time. My family is my top priority, and I respect that for others, so I rarely send emails or call my team in the evening or on weekends. Second, pay attention to how you transition from the end of a workweek into a weekend or holiday break. Personally, if I don't end every workweek with some sort of acknowledgment or evaluation of how that week went, then I won't be able to enjoy the weekend. I'll be thinking about the week, my work, and the week ahead, and I won't be fully present with my family or friends. I've heard similar things from employees. This is why, during my first frontline leadership job at Honeywell, in a factory in San Diego, I wanted every employee to know how we were doing at the end of the week. On Fridays, I'd recap the week—close out initiatives and highlight our objectives—and then specifically call out what we would work on the next week, so employees didn't need to worry or wonder about it over the weekend.

Give people permission to take a break and enjoy other parts of life. This might seem small, but it's one of the most important things you can do as a leader. All of the people your employees impact are impacted by you as well. When you see the whole person, you can have a positive impact on your employees' lives, as well as the lives of their entire families. You empower them to grow as parents, partners, and members of their communities. They might never meet you, but in a small way, you've made a positive contribution to their lives. That's huge. At the same time, you have created a culture where people buy in with enthusiasm, are eager to work their hardest, and invest in the company that's invested in them.

Coach Rather Than Direct

Empowerment is an ongoing process of learning and development for your employees, and you have the opportunity to create the conditions that allow them to continue to grow. This requires a shift in mindset, from thinking like a manager to thinking like a coach. A manager usually will delegate tasks, lead meetings, collect input, make strategic decisions, and so on. All of this is important, but an overly controlling management style will stifle your employees' development. They will become so accustomed to you providing road maps or scheduling every aspect of their day that it will weaken their ability to think creatively on their own. Worse, they won't have the time or energy necessary to survey the landscape—one that they, being on the front lines, know better than *you*—and discover process issues, much less the solutions to those problems.

Instead of micromanaging your employees, empower them by providing clear direction and guidance on priorities. Set goals that align with company objectives, and then coach your employees. Gain an understanding of their challenges and enable them to work it out on their own. Be available to answer their questions, but give them the space to make decisions. In doing so, you gift them with the opportunity to practice on their own, to make mistakes, and to learn from these, so that they can grow.

Any sports fan knows that there are hundreds of different coaching styles, all of which can be successful. You can find success with the hyper-professional Zen of the NBA's Phil Jackson or the high-energy exuberance of the NFL's Pete Carroll. No matter your style, there are two fundamentals upon which any successful coaching strategy is built. The first is setting a high, clear bar for your team members, which shows that you believe in them. The second is doing everything you can to help them achieve that standard, which demonstrates your unwavering commitment to their success.

First, the bar. Set specific goals with your team members. If the goal is quality, discuss what quality looks like for their position, what it looks like for the people supporting them, and what can be measured daily or weekly that would indicate how well they're meeting that objective. When they know which metrics they're striving to improve, they can see more opportunities. They can find and fix design flaws in a product. They can say, "Hey, maybe the material we're getting isn't high quality enough." Or they can find places to streamline the supply chain, to automate processes. To take it a step further, encourage them to set their own goals. This will help them establish ownership and increase motivation to achieve those goals.

The high bar you set should include more than just quantitative individual goals. Be sure to make it also about the unreachable peak, the quantitative and qualitative successes, that the entire company is working toward. But the highest expectations in the world won't help you coach your teams if you don't help them achieve these ambitious goals. In fact, there are few things more toxic than a leader who asks a lot from a team, and then makes it almost impossible for the team to deliver. If you do that, your employees will feel like you're just setting them up to fail.

On the other hand, if you set a high bar with your teams and then support them by investing time and resources, you show that you believe in them. This belief alone is empowering, and makes employees feel valued, challenged, and excited at work, even before they start to see their goals come to fruition. When, with your support, they achieve those goals, that moment massively increases their own confidence and sense of empowerment within the organization.

You can support their development in a myriad of ways. The most obvious are new training and skill development programs, or giving them the resources (e.g., money, technology, time, access, information) that they need to succeed. For example, you could share aspects of your experience, or help them develop relationships within the company and the industry, so that they can expand their personal networks and learn from their peers.

A quick note: You can only ask your employees to do all this extra work to continuously learn if you make an equal, consistent effort to grow yourself. They are all experts at their jobs, and you can learn just as much from them as they do from you.

Invest time in developing yourself, to embody a commitment to continuous learning that will inspire others to follow.

All of this is in stark contrast to the legacy top-down model, which requires employees to fit a mold that can be plugged into the machine—people who are expected to execute orders without contributing input of their own. With frontline leadership, you're disrupting this model by challenging your employees, demonstrating your belief in them, and helping them excel.

Reward Positive Behavior

A vital part of successful coaching is to ensure that you reward positive behavior. It seems obvious, but in large organizations, it can sometimes be easy to misinterpret a situation and react negatively to what is a positive development. For example, suppose an employee who reports to you rises to your challenge, sees a process problem, and fixes it. Another employee might feel like the first person stepped on that employee's toes, overreached from his or her position, whatever it might be. The second employee reports the first employee to his or her boss, and that other manager comes to you and says, "Hey, your employee is stepping out of his lane. He's creating conflict with my team. Can you talk to him?"

What you do here matters, as a wrong move can have tremendous consequences and undermine your own efforts toward building frontline leadership. Before reacting to the information you received from the other manager, it's vital that you assess whether your employee really was acting in a rude or counterproductive way, or whether he or she was doing what you asked and it triggered a negative emotional response in the other employee. If your employee was doing what you asked and contributed a good improvement to or shift in the process, then you commend that person for that. You want to reward the effort and, importantly, *acknowledge the improvement*. At the same time, it might also be worthwhile to take this opportunity to coach the employee on how to work across silos in a way that doesn't undermine others. Change is hard, so understanding everyone impacted and engaging them early is important.

If, on the other hand, your employee was way out of line and made a mistake that somehow made the process worse, you still don't need to take a disciplinary approach. Obviously, have a conversation. Help your employee learn from the mistake and extrapolate from it, but—and this is key—still commend the person for taking that initiative, for trying something new. You want to empower effort in the direction of your goals in an environment where people challenge each other constructively.

In either situation, if you just had a knee-jerk reaction and moved straight to disciplinary action against the employee for moving across silos, especially after you'd explicitly encouraged employees to do so, you'll breed bitterness in your workforce. That employee will conclude, "OK, I tried to go above and beyond, I tried to fill the gaps, but I'm the one who got punished for it. *I'll never do that again!*" Then you'll have something much worse than a disempowered employee: a disengaged, resentful one.

Left unchecked, this can quickly turn toxic for the entire organization. One disgruntled or disengaged employee will vent to other coworkers who will then spread the story of this managerial slight throughout the ranks. For this reason, it is vital to remain consistent in your expectations and reward structure. It's even better if you can prevent these situations from occurring in the first place.

For frontline leadership to truly empower employees, everyone on your team needs to understand the importance of working together, as one unit, toward a common goal. The type of corrosive infighting, in which one employee feels *threatened* by the actions of another, doesn't occur naturally. It comes from a competitive culture that is so focused on individual performance that employees are incentivized to gain an inside track on a promotion or a raise, even if it means undercutting their coworkers instead of focusing on how they can help the company grow as a whole. In fact, trying to switch to a flat leadership structure in this kind of environment can cause catastrophic damage, as people will use their newfound freedom and power to stay within their silos, promote themselves, and undermine the team as a whole.

To prevent this, make sure that everyone works as a team, and that starts with fostering empathy and connection with one another. Effective communication relies on more than speaking and listening; it relies on a true understanding of others and their viewpoints. Often, in large organizations, uncontructive rivalries spring up between different departments. Marketing thinks its job is harder than sales, who think its job is harder than fulfillment, and on it goes. When this happens, communication between groups on how they can work on coordinated and integrated growth and development becomes nearly impossible. Of course, work in each silo poses its own unique challenges, and oftentimes a failure in one arena can affect the others. In a toxic environment, these communication breakdowns breed resentment that fractures the team. I've found that the best way to avoid this is to foster understanding, to help your employees see the world through their workers' eyes. When you set the example as a mindful, empathetic leader, it goes a long way toward cultivating this interdepartmental connection. Use a shadowing or job rotation program, where people from one department either shadow or take over for someone in another department. To generate empathy and build mutual understanding, there's nothing like walking in someone else's shoes.

Roll Up Your Sleeves and Chip In

In order for a company to truly be one team, everybody has to embrace that value, including, and especially, the executives. Any executive who wants to lead from the front lines needs to consistently spend time there. If executives stay on the sidelines, it breeds an us-versus-them dynamic between management and employees, and makes people believe that your priorities aren't aligned with theirs. When you go to the front lines of the teams you lead, roll up your sleeves and chip in. It helps build relationships and empathy with your employees, which will lead to better decision-making, allow them to feel seen and truly valued. It also makes you more approachable.

My first leadership role was as a manufacturing supervisor in a casting shop that made pressure switches for thermostats. Every day, I'd go out to the shop floor right after our first meeting and see where I could be of the most help. Of course, there were days when I was overwhelmed with work and needed to spend time writing a business case to support the purchase of new equipment or creating budgets for the next quarter. But effective leaders find the time to build their teams, create repeatable processes, and delegate tasks, all of which increase efficiency and provide opportunities for your team to grow. When you have a well-trained team working in sync, you can dedicate more time to the most important responsibility of a leader: coaching and developing your team members. Working on the front lines is one of the best ways to do that. It enables you to role model responsibility, hard work, and humility, and it also builds essential trust between you and the people on the front lines.

To be successful, you have to go with an authentic desire to help, and with ample humility. Recognize that the people on the front lines know how to do their jobs better than you do.

Make sure that you don't go there with an attitude of "Well, I'm the boss, so it's my job to know how to pack boxes and write code better than you, so let me show you how it's done." That approach will have the opposite effect—people will see you as condescending and will most likely end up less engaged. Just go and see how you can help, and do it.

In that first leadership role, the factory floor was as dirty as manufacturing gets. There were metal chips and machine fluids all over the place. I asked, "How can I help?" and somebody said, "Grab a mop." So, I did, and I did the same the other times I went there, until eventually, I didn't have to ask.

Spending time working side by side with my team, I began to see the challenges they faced in their day-to-day work. I noticed whether they had the proper tools or enough supplies. I observed how their direct supervisors behaved and what their leadership styles were. I could tell if we had the right number of employees to do the job safely, and see if the workplace environment was safe and clean.

This practice has become an essential part of my leadership strategy. It's something you can start doing tomorrow to kick off the transition to frontline leadership, though you can take it even further than just mopping the floor.

While CEO of Aviall, I spent time either shadowing or directly working at every frontline job, just so I could understand what life was like in each position. Then I reflected on how to make those jobs more meaningful, how to better communicate our strategy to that team, and how to support employees to develop and grow on their own. The more time you can spend on the front lines, the better. The front line is where change actually happens and where new ideas are implemented.

On top of that, going to the front lines can give you an excellent way to measure the effectiveness of your decision-making and communication as a leader. You can find out whether your employees understand where the company is going and the reasoning behind the various decisions that have been made.

Whenever you or someone in the upper levels of management makes a major decision—where to open a plant, whether to shut down a product line, when to break into a new market, etc.—a companywide *narrative* springs up around that decision. If you honestly communicate the reasoning behind it, exhibit transparency, and rely on the relationships you've already built with your employees, then they'll believe what you tell them. But if you're not open and upfront in sharing information, or lack a strong relationship with your employees, they'll disregard whatever you say and generate their own narratives, which will erode trust and undermine performance.

Go to the front lines and build those relationships. Make it your informal office, and try to break down as many barriers to participation and access as possible. Make sure that your commitment to working alongside those on the front lines is more than cosmetic, or your attempt at creating frontline leaders will fail.

That's why, back in that first leadership job, I mopped, even if I was alone and no one was watching. During my last week, before I left for a new role within a different division at Honeywell, I was out on the floor mopping, and one of the guys on the shift found me there. He was stunned, and said, "Eric, what are you doing? You know you're leaving, right? You don't have to do that anymore."

I knew that. But I did it anyway because the floor needed to be cleaned and I had made a commitment to my team to work beside them to do what needed to be done.

2

KNOW YOUR PURPOSE AND LIVE IT

I n 2009, while I was serving as the vice president of supply chain management at L3 Communications, the U.S. Armed Forces asked us to accelerate deployment of a new aircraft that would provide tremendous protection to troops overseas. Because this aircraft was being designed and built with the ability to save lives, each day of delay could mean the deaths of our men and women who serve. In the months after receiving that assignment, L3 became the single most focused organization I have ever seen. Everyone, from the CEO down, committed everything he or she could to expedite the process. Company badges, titles, civilian/military distinctions—none of this mattered. Everyone was aligned, engaged, and innovating to deliver the plane.

Under normal circumstances, that standard process would take several years. We completed and deployed that aircraft in eight months. Casualty numbers immediately dropped. In recognition of the quality and speed of our work, Robert Gates, then secretary of defense, visited our site to personally congratulate the team.

We only achieved this accomplishment because we all connected so thoroughly to our purpose, which was to save lives.

Even before this specific mission, everyone at L3 already felt connected to our purpose, put in extra effort, and collaborated freely. The new initiative pushed all of that into overdrive. Any internal competitiveness or posturing for promotions that might have existed before disappeared. We all pooled our knowledge into one unified effort to find the best solution.

While not every project deals so explicitly in matters of life and death, you can still create an environment in which employees work with as much focus, determination, and collaboration as I witnessed at L3 during that time. It all comes back to purpose. Every decision we make as individuals, every investment in time, and every career move should be grounded in our purpose. It's what gives us direction, fulfillment, and, ultimately, joy.

The same is true in business: a company's purpose will guide the direction in which it needs to grow. It's also been proven that companies with an authentic connection to a purpose, especially one that makes a positive impact in the world, are more profitable over the long term.* This connection to purpose fortifies brand identity, fosters trust with consumers, and, because everyone wants to work in service of a higher purpose, helps attract and retain top talent.

An impeccable example is the King Arthur Baking Company, previously known as King Arthur Flour. Founded in Boston in 1790 to sell English-milled flour, it identified its purpose to "inspire connections and community by spreading the joy of baking" and used that purpose to create a sustainable advantage in the market. In its effort to develop local communities, in the 1820s, the company transitioned from importing English flour

---

* Jenn Lim, "A Study Says Your Company's 'Purpose' Can Increase Returns By 400 Percent. Here's How to Create One That Works," Inc.com, December 20, 2018, https:// www.inc.com/jenn-lim/a-study-says-your-companys-purpose-can-increase-returns-by -400-percent-heres-how-to-create-one-that-works.html.

to milling flour from American wheat. In the centuries since, guided by its purpose—and its belief that everyone can bake and that baking and breaking bread brings people together—the company has grown beyond its initial product. It produces cookbooks and instructional videos and offers in-person baking classes. It has built a community of bakers around a commitment to the core values of inclusion, diversity, equity, social impact, and sustainability, and manifests those values in everything the company does. It donates the extra food produced from its cooking lessons to food banks and shelters, provides financial incentives for employees to carpool, and installed solar panels at every work site. In 2004, when owners Frank and Brinna Sands retired, they wanted to ensure that the company maintained its commitment to purpose and community, so they sold it to their workers. The company is 100 percent employee owned and still guided by its core purpose and values. This purpose has become its brand identity, and its impact is clear: it has been recognized by *Vermont Business Magazine* as one of the Best Places to Work in Vermont every year from 2006 (the year of the award's inception) through 2020.

Not every company grows as gracefully as King Arthur Flour. The challenge that companies face as they grow is the need to convince a larger and more diverse group of people to believe in and support their purpose. This is especially true if a company wants to implement a frontline leadership strategy, as it requires orienting toward the organization's purpose—not relying on the organizational chart for direction. Although organizational charts play an essential part in clarifying roles and responsibilities, establishing authority, and supporting compliance requirements, they don't encourage innovation. If everyone tries to obey the chart—doing only what each job describes—the result will often lead to institutionalizing the status quo. Of course, it's good to do one's job according to the description. But, and especially in an organization with frontline leadership, everyone should think beyond the chart, strive for greater impact, and look for ways to better serve the mission. Purpose should act as the compass to drive and guide every action that solves problems for customers and allows the company to compete and grow. It's the reason your company exists, what you're uniquely positioned to do, and what the world would miss if you were gone.

If you attempt to implement frontline leadership without a clear sense of purpose that permeates the organization, your newly empowered workforce might go running off in a hundred different directions, killing productivity and undermining corporate health. But if everyone understands the main goal, then all can move toward it together. This, of course, is easier said than done. And, like everything else, the best first step is at the micro level: by getting clarity on how you define *your* purpose. Once you've done that, the next step is to help each employee connect to the company's purpose.

Step #1: Define Your Personal Purpose

Defining your personal purpose is a gateway to putting your values in action. It's what gives life meaning. It guides your choices and creates an opportunity to make a personal commitment to a cause, to a lifestyle, to building beneficial habits and routines. But purpose, like values, constantly evolves and changes, as we learn more, understand diverse perspectives, and gain experience by moving through different stages of life. So make a habit of reflecting on your purpose, what matters to you, and how your perspective has changed over time. For example, I have long understood my core values, and they have always played a part in my purpose. But my purpose has changed over time, evolving through out my life and career. During my time as CEO of Aviall, I reached a point of success at which I realized that I needed to focus more on serving others, on paying forward all of the resources that other people had invested in me. The next time I sat down to reflect on my purpose and goals, it became immediately clear that I wanted to make a positive impact for more people by creating opportunities for those who don't have the same access to resources and support that I do. This was in alignment with several of my core values—optimism, serving others, hard work—and it became a new objective, a new iteration of my purpose, that arose in that moment. I followed that impulse, and eventually, founded SUMMi7.

Perfect clarity is impossible to achieve, but doesn't need to stop you from moving forward. More reflection can uncover deeper layers of meaning, motivation, and nuance to your values and worldview, which is why it is so important to continue learning. It can help you identify what matters most, the change you most want to see in the world, enabling you to build a career around that. You can find a company that aligns with what you care about and a vocation that lets you make an impact by leveraging your strengths. Then you're on the path to a rewarding, meaningful life.

Step #2: Connect Employees to the Company's Purpose

Purpose, as defined by William Damon, director of the Stanford Center on Adolescence, is "a long-term, forward-looking intention to accomplish aims that are both meaningful to the self and of consequence to the world beyond the self." For a company, that means that purpose must have some significance beyond profit. Your company needs to have a concrete improvement that it wants to make in the world. Then you can connect each individual employee's role to that purpose, and give employees the space to fulfill their responsibilities in a way that feels authentic to them. The result will be a more inclusive and unified organization. A higher purpose unites people and helps them connect despite cultural differences. It encourages people to work across cultural barriers and recognize that people with different perspectives can make a unique and valuable contribution.

In the twenty-first century, this orientation toward inclusivity is more important than ever before. Business is increasingly global, with more multinational corporations, customers, and problems to solve than at any prior point in history. Whether a company acknowledges it or not, we are now part of a global ecosystem, and through the news and social media, employees can see the impact that events in faraway places have on their lives, whether at the gas pump or in the technology they use. Companies have to respond to this global environment, and to do that effectively, they need to bring in diverse perspectives, to encourage employees from different backgrounds to come into work authentically and leverage their unique points of view to find new solutions. That starts with a powerful, unifying narrative about a higher mission that everyone connects to and strives toward.

Connecting employees to the company's purpose starts when employees first join an organization. During my years leading Aviall, I made sure that each employee understood the impact he or she made from day one. We were the world's largest aerospace parts distributor. We had more than 20,000 customers and 40 locations, and shipped up to 15,000 line items a day. An operation of this scale and complexity requires a great deal of administrative labor—to plan, buy, receive, stock, pick, and ship all of the parts. It's exactly the type of environment where employees might easily lose sight of the company's purpose. Boxing a part, printing paperwork, and staging on a dock for shipment hundreds of times each day can seem mundane. But as leaders of the company, we knew that some of those parts may help repair a medivac helicopter that saves lives, support a wheel repair for a C-17 on a humanitarian mission, or allow airlines to maintain their schedules and bring people to their loved ones.

To enrich our new employees' understanding of our narrative, one of my fellow leaders or I would attend every new hire orientation. We would introduce ourselves in a transparent, authentic way, explaining our personal motivators and the way we connected to the company. Then we would invite the new hires to share, to talk about who they are and what they care about. After starting to build a personal connection, you can begin to discuss how your purpose interacts with the company's purpose. You cannot invert this process—if you don't take the time to get to know people, then the new employees might ignore you when you start talking about the company's vision. Because we had established a dialogue of listening and getting to know each other, whenever we started talking about the company's purpose, the new employees were more likely to participate. Often, they would ask insightful questions from an external point of view, which helped me gain new clarity on the company's vision as well as my own.

We would also invite new employees to stand up and share more about their new jobs. For example, one introduced herself, saying, "Hi, I'm Jolene and I'm working in a warehouse in Australia. Just started last week; happy to be here."

That gave me a chance to connect her role directly with something she could see, so I said, "Welcome, Jolene. Well, let me tell you, Australia is a $50 million business for us. It's the biggest general aviation market outside of the United States. When you look out your window, every plane that flies by has a part on it that comes from us."

In doing this, I'm hoping to help her understand how her position fits into our broader mission as a company and, ultimately, makes a difference in the world. When she starts to work, and when the daily repetition of the job sets in, her connection to the company purpose will be stronger, and she'll be able to find purpose in her daily actions knowing that she plays a role in supporting all the aircraft flying overhead. Of course, maintaining strong connection between people and purpose requires continuous effort. There are other key elements of leadership, such as transparency and removing complexity, which I'll discuss later, that will help maintain that connection.

In these meetings and in my other responsibilities as CEO, I always worked to instill an optimistic outlook among our employees. Optimism operates as a powerful tool for connecting to purpose. To feel inspired to work toward a higher goal, people need not only to believe that the goal is worth pursuing but that it is possible. Former Secretary of State Colin Powell once said, "Perpetual optimism is a force multiplier." I've seen this throughout my entire life and career, starting with my mother, who woke up each morning with an optimistic view of our future. Optimism isn't a utopian, unrealistic view. Rather, optimism is the belief that the future you envision can be achieved. That belief will power you through the obstacles and failures you'll inevitably face. To instill optimism as a leader of a company, focus on the upside of what is possible, and then believe in and support your leaders to achieve that upside.

There's one other strategy that I've used with great success to keep people connected to purpose. Almost every company changes its official purpose statement from time to time. Companies do this because their purpose has shifted or they want to try to find a more powerful way to express the same core idea. The latter is why we decided to revamp our purpose statement at Aviall. We wanted it to encapsulate all of the forms of flight that we supported. So we organized a contest: any employee at Aviall could submit a purpose statement describing why we exist. The contest encouraged employees to reflect on what they were doing at work. Those hours of reflection boosted every employee's connection to and understanding of our purpose, regardless of whether we chose their statement. Eventually, three third-shift warehouse team members landed on a sentence that perfectly encapsulated our purpose: "Proudly keeping the world in flight."

This became our north star. It allowed us to talk to all the important missions of our industry and feel proud of the support we provided. After adopting this new purpose statement, we worked to build our culture around serving customers and supporting their vital missions. We launched the Customer Connect program, which brought employees out to see our customers at work and brought customers in to talk at employee meetings. We also shared customer spotlights in our weekly and monthly communications. This supported a brand pillar of our company: the ability to provide flexible and innovative solutions to our customers because we understand them, live their problems, share their purpose, and align everything we do to support them.

This contest also proved that our company led from the front lines. In a multibillion-dollar, complicated, 85-year-old organization, our purpose statement came from the people who were out there getting it done everyday: three warehouse workers—not an external firm, not the executive team. That indicated that our leadership was purpose-driven. It meant we had a clear view of the customer and the impact we created at all levels of the organization, and that we incorporated enough transparency into our operations that every employee understood our organization and how each employee fit in it.

Purpose Lost, Purpose Regained

Sometimes a company can lose track of its purpose. I've seen this happen most often in the context of three challenges:

1. Organizational growth, which requires a larger group of people to connect to the purpose
2. Stagnation, slow erosion of clarity and focus over time
3. New strategies, expansion into adjacent products or markets that don't align with the company's original purpose

In each case, you must work quickly to reorient to your purpose and organize your systems around it, before irreparable damage is done. Let's look at each cause and ways to address it.

Challenge #1: Organizational Growth

Almost every successful company starts with a founder or a group of founders who all want to serve customers in a specific way. Often, the founders feel a more powerful connection to the company's purpose than most subsequent employees do because the company is born of the founders' personal purpose. If the founders succeed in positioning their company within the market, they will need to hire teams. But if a company isn't careful, each new hire and each new layer of management between the founders and the front lines might pull the company out of alignment with its purpose. In most top-down leadership systems, it doesn't take long before new employees feel like they're joining a large, complex organization where it's difficult to see how their work and ideas fit in, or how their contributions impact the customer, never mind the world. In those scenarios, even the most enthusiastically engaged employees' connection to purpose will wane. The result is that people start to go through the motions, which allows legacy processes to become entrenched and causes the company to lose its competitive advantage, often indicated by eroding profit margins.

However, although new employees may not have the same connection to a company's purpose as the founders, you can still create inspiration by pulling them into your vision. A company can achieve this by creating an inclusive environment, where each person is encouraged to bring his or her unique ideas and perspectives to the table. Those unique ideas expand the impact beyond what the founder alone could achieve. That expanded impact will, in turn, create new avenues through which employees can see a vision that they are now a part of. King Arthur Baking Company is instructive here. As that company grew and brought on new generations of employees, it expanded its impact, transforming from a flour importer, to a miller of American wheat, and finally into a baking institution. Now, new employees might feel the most motivated by the communities King Arthur creates through their cooking classes. After two full centuries of change, the connection to purpose is just as strong as when the company was founded, arguably stronger. The chapters that follow in this book will help identify and remove the obstacles that prevent employees from connecting with purpose as a company grows.

Challenge #2: Stagnation

The other factor in the erosion of connection to purpose is time. This is especially common within the most successful companies, the behemoths that have become the bedrocks of their industries and seen many tides of leadership that have come and gone. When a company becomes entrenched—when it is so large and so well known that it seems almost invulnerable or when it operates the same way no matter who worked there—is when a company's connection to its purpose is most fragile. Not only will most new hires never meet the founder, the founder might not even still be alive. And it's not just new hires, but everyone, including top-level executives, who run the risk of forgetting why the company exists.

For example, Aviall was founded in 1932. When I was CEO, we'd already had more than 80 years of history, during which Aviall saw countless transformations, including being acquired by Boeing. The tendency, one that we needed to fight against, was to simply think of Aviall as an airplane parts distribution company, one aspect of the larger Boeing supply chain. Aviall's true purpose is "Proudly keeping the world in flight." It's about connecting the world, allowing the modern miracle of air travel to change people's lives every single day. I needed to keep the true purpose in mind at all times and to help employees understand it as well. Without that constant vigilance, it would have been easy to let the question "How can we best deliver airplane parts?" guide our decision-making, instead of "How can we proudly keep the world in flight?" The first question might help us find ways to ship parts faster, but to answer the second question required us to better understand other problems we could help customers solve beyond just delivering a part. It led us to integrate our systems and processes with customers' maintenance systems to share data, kit parts, preposition material, offer lower cost alternatives, and provide streamlined paperwork to improve the handling and traceability of components. This distinction might seem trivial, but at the end of the day, what you use as a guiding principle will have a dramatic effect on how your organization operates. If you don't stay true to your purpose and that of the company, you'll quickly get pulled in a direction that you probably did not intend to go.

For instance, one of my early consulting clients left her corporate Human Resources job to start her own recruitment firm. She built her company into quite a successful entity, but she felt that there was something holding her employees back from taking the next step, which is why she came to us. We talked about purpose, and early in the conversation, she said that her purpose was making sure she found the right talent for the company. To me, this sounded a little too much like describing Aviall's purpose as "Delivering airplane parts." So I asked her, "Why did you leave your secure, high-paying job at that big company in the first place? What motivated you to take that risk?"

She replied, "I wanted to help companies build stronger, diverse teams."

That's her real purpose, and it's much bigger than merely recruiting. If your goal is to find what traditional thinking mistakenly considers the "best talent," then you're going to be bringing in a lot of Ivy League grads and trying to hire from other companies and networks that are familiar to you. But if your goal is to help diverse teams work together and create an inclusive environment that leverages diversity to devise solutions to the complicated challenges of the twenty-first century, then you'll expand your search beyond these traditional and limiting sources for top talent. Doing so will enable you to discover people who *really are* the best, even if they didn't come from the most prestigious institutions.

You'll also begin to work in partnership with the clients, first to understand how their current team and culture operate, and then to determine the talent that would best complement the existing infrastructure. The basic company mechanism stays the same, the primary service (i.e., recruiting) stays the same, but the operation, the goal, and the target shift. It becomes more specific, with greater differentiation from competitors, and allows you to offer more creative solutions.

After that discussion, the already successful founder went back to her office, shared that revelation with her team, and later called me to say that everyone left the meeting feeling invigorated. Increasing effectiveness among diverse teams is a goal that inspires people, much more so than just "finding the right talent." This newfound specificity of purpose will help her business in a myriad of other ways. As a firm that will work with companies to develop diverse teams, which, studies have shown, improves innovation and outcomes while simultaneously promoting cohesion, she'll be able to differentiate herself from all of the other recruitment firms that headhunt at top schools.* This differentiation will help her to identify and seek out her ideal customers, as well as help her ideal customers find her.

My client didn't have to reach too far back into the past to rediscover her purpose—only a few years into her personal history. At Aviall, I didn't have that luxury. Instead, for our eighty-fifth anniversary, we commissioned a team to put together a report on our founding. They revived the story of founder Edward "Doc" Booth, a retired army aviator who, after completing his service, decided that he wanted to help

---

* Stuart R. Levine, "Diversity Confirmed to Boost Innovation and Financial Results," *Forbes*, May 18, 2021, https://www.forbes.com/sites/forbesinsights/2020/01/15/diversity-confirmed-to-boost-innovation-and-financial-results/?sh=3695ffaec4a.

future generations of pilots, so he created the company that later became Aviall. It was born of camaraderie, a commitment to service—both to the nation and to the community—and, importantly, the need to maintain safety. The team wrote all of this up and compiled it in a book, and we gave a copy to each of the employees at the anniversary celebration. We also invited Doc Booth's granddaughter to join us for that special occasion, which strengthened our connection to our purpose even further.

By tapping into the original inspiration for Aviall and rein-troducing that story into the hearts and minds of our employees, we reignited the fire of our culture.

Challenge #3: New Strategies

Sometimes, a growing company will experience a shift in its purpose due to opportunities that pull it out of alignment from its original purpose. This doesn't need to become a problem, but if the leadership isn't aware of the shift or doesn't know how to realign the company, it can result in painful misalignment. Take, for instance, another one of my consulting clients who runs a successful financial advising company that manages portfolios for a range of businesses and individuals.

She'd reached a point where her original goal—financial independence for herself and others—no longer felt as fulfill-ing, so she decided to expand the scope of her operations. She began to offer training to teach people how to manage their finances. This new possibility created a degree of uncertainty. It also required her to reevaluate her purpose, so that she could ensure that her expanded offerings were aligned with it. Our conversation went something like this:

"What are you really trying to do?"

"I want to create financial stability for women and especially women in transition."

"Why?"

"I want to help women advance into leadership positions, so they can create a positive influence for others."

"Tell me more."

"I want to create opportunities to position more women on boards because I think that'll create stronger, more inclusive companies."

That was her purpose. When she was able to articulate it, the connection for her was so strong that it became emotional for both of us. What she wants to do is help women move into the next phase of their careers. Most of her clients are female executives, and the next step for them after financial independence is to get a seat at the table in the boardrooms of different companies and organizations. That's where they can influence broad and lasting change. My client realized that she wants to help women achieve that because, as studies have shown, companies with female board members not only increase their profits but also tend to operate with a broader view of shareholder value to include the good of society.* She realized that this is how she can make a global impact within her same organization.

She left our meeting with a renewed focus on the few key strategies she should prioritize to most effectively achieve her expanded purpose. It also helped her to reevaluate the entire company. Now, instead of just managing her clients' portfolios, she's entering into a deeper partnership, coaching them through the process of becoming financially independent, and later becoming an influential member of a board.

------

* Jie Chen, Woon Sau Leung, Wei Song, and Marc Goergen, "Research: When Women Are on Boards, Male CEOs Are Less Overconfident," *Harvard Business Review,* September 12, 2019, https://hbr.org/2019/09/research-when-women-are-on-boards-male-ceos-are-less-overconfident

She reevaluated the expectations for each role of every one of her team members, and started to question how she could better lead her employees. Then, she studied the services they offered to see where they needed to expand to achieve their new purpose. She began working *on* the business, instead of just *in* the business. But she could only do that once she saw her new purpose and aligned her business to match it. We both grew out of that short engagement and left recommitted to purpose and energized by the potential to make a greater impact on the world.

Purpose and Partnership

Purpose alone will not ensure a company's success. You also need a robust community of support, drawn from both within and outside the company. Without this community, without strong partnership, you'll inevitably run into challenges that are difficult to overcome on your own. You'll know where you want to go, but get stuck in the attempt to get there. On the flip side, if you have powerful partnerships, but no purpose, you won't make meaningful strides either, as you'll have no clear destination.

The good news is that partnership and purpose feed one another. You can use a common purpose as a rallying call to bring together a diverse group of people, and partnership fuels the drive toward a common goal. To create a culture where frontline leadership is possible, you need both.

If you're able to foster partnership with purpose, then when your company inevitably hits a bump in the road, your people will be inclined to attack the problems and work on them as a team. They'll do this because they each know their purpose, they feel connected to it, and they're in a community of people who truly care about one another. With strong relationships, purpose, and trust, even major problems can bring people together.

In turn, partnership helps a common purpose evolve. For instance, one of the newer challenges facing aviation is aircraft recycling. Aviation grew and evolved rapidly in the twentieth and twenty-first centuries, creating a large number of aircraft that phase out of use each year that we need to dispose of in a sustainable, responsible way. As in other relatively youthful industries, such as electronics and automobiles, for many years, aviation lacked a standardized procedure for disassembling aircraft.

To remedy this, 11 major aviation companies created the Aircraft Fleet Recycling Association. With members in Africa, Europe, and North America, this group focuses on bringing together aviation companies at every point in the supply chain (manufacturers, distributors, airlines, etc.) to promote environmental best practices, regulatory excellence, and sustainable developments in aircraft disassembly, salvaging, and recycling. From this partnership has come an inspired new commitment to a specific purpose—environmental sustainability—throughout the industry.

These sorts of partnerships develop purpose and allow companies to solve bigger and more complicated problems than they could on their own. For best results, companies should consider creating partnerships with six key stakeholder groups:

- Shareholders
- Employees
- Customers
- Suppliers
- Community partners
- Industry affiliates

Shareholders

Shareholders are the owners of a company who invest their capital to receive an expected return or outcome. The board of directors is the committee that provides governance over how the company is managed in accordance with shareholder expectations and governing documents such as bylaws. Historically, these expectations have been purely financial, managing how capital is deployed in alignment with risk and return scenarios.

In the late 2010s, many well-respected journals, both in the business world and the mainstream, published articles arguing against the expansion of shareholder influence on companies. The argument was that most firms prioritize short-term profits and returns for shareholders, often at the expense of worker and consumer safety, environmental sustainability, and the greater good of society. Fortune 500 companies took note. In 2019, the Business Roundtable, an organization founded in 1978 that includes the CEOs of leading US companies such as 3M, Amazon, Apple, Johnson & Johnson, P&G, Starbucks, and Walmart, updated their official statement on the Purpose of a Corporation. Whereas in each previous statement the Roundtable endorsed shareholder primacy, the 2019 statement declared the Purpose of a Corporation is to serve not only traditional shareholders but also the interests of employees, suppliers, customers, and the community equally. In doing so, more than 180 CEOs of the largest corporations committed to a purpose beyond financial returns, addressing issues such as climate change, racial equity and justice, and education in support of an "economy that serves us all."*

---

* Business Roundtable, "Business Roundtable Redefines the Purpose of a Corporation to Promote 'An Economy That Serves All Americans'," Business Roundtable, August 19, 2019, https://www.businessroundtable.org/business-roundtable-redefines-the-purpose-of-a-corporation-to-promote-an-economy-that-serves-all-americans.

This is an important first step, which acknowledges the unsustainability of the practices of the twentieth century. But all of these companies need to show their continued commitment to these ideals, which will require years of effort and vigilance. They should break down old barriers to participation, encourage inclusion, and grow in alignment with this commitment. The concepts in this book provide an outline for exactly how to do that.

An important way to follow through on that commitment is to improve how companies partner with shareholders. Shareholders will always exist for publicly traded firms, which means that companies need to enlist their shareholders in their commitment to responsible and sustainable growth.

Although we have yet to see the long-term impact the statement will have, it's provided an opportunity for large, established organizations to expand their purpose to include economic, environmental, and social good in alignment with their values and core capabilities. At Aviall, this included the social causes that we supported in alignment with our values, such as investing in education and veterans' outreach, along with supporting nonprofits such as the North Texas Food Bank, which runs a large distribution operation that can benefit from our operating best practices. Similar to Microsoft donating technical support and equipment to schools, LinkedIn providing specialized support to veterans to advance their careers, and Unilever setting targets and helping their suppliers meet environmental sustainability in the communities in which they operate, companies can apply their know-how to help others. In doing so, they will connect their purpose with a broad set of stakeholders far beyond the financial statements.

Another indicator of progress is the large investment firms that are also looking to put more money into businesses that embrace purpose as a vehicle for social good. BlackRock, currently the worlds largest asset manager, now only invests in companies with a strong sustainability plan.* As we continue to discover just how interconnected the world is and how our actions on the corporate level can support or hinder the well-being of billions of people, investors are trying to allocate funds in a more conscious way. They recognize that if a company behaves irresponsibly, then the community gets hurt, and the community is its customers.

If you are a founder or leader in a relatively young organization looking to scale, then you have the opportunity to build purpose into your strategy, operating goals, and culture right from the start. Early on in your company's development, as you're looking for investors, research the firms/individuals that you are pitching to ahead of time and be transparent about your aspirations beyond profits. If you believe that most people want to contribute something beyond themselves and most companies underutilize their potential to do so, then you can see how setting goals for broader impact—such as any combination of the 17 UN Sustainable Development Goals†—will create a higher purpose that lasts beyond business cycles.

Employees

Partnering with your employees begins with listening to them, and then following up on what you hear. At Aviall, we did this through regular roundtables with employees, to get the pulse of the organization. At one of them, an employee said, "Hey, I get it. We do something important here, but a lot of us are really

---

* Blackrock, "Our approach to sustainability," July 2020, accessed May 18, 2021, https://www.blackrock.com/corporate/literature/publication/our-commitment-to-sustainability-full-report.pdf.
† United Nations Foundation, "Sustainable Development Goals," https://unfoundation.org/what-we-do/issues/sustainable-development-goals/.

inspired by what we're doing in our community, such as supporting local schools and developing the next generation of leaders."

In response to this comment, we added the following to our objectives: to help our employees find their own purpose and to support them in engaging with their communities in their areas of passion. Shortly after, we found out that one of our employees was the father of a child with juvenile diabetes. Every year he participated in the Juvenile Diabetes Research Foundation walk to raise money and awareness. That year, when he went to walk, about 50 coworkers from Aviall accompanied him. His purpose became our purpose, and we partnered with him to make a difference on an issue that mattered to him. These efforts have grown into dozens of events each year led by employees, creating a positive impact in the communities in which we live and work. Our support helps lift communities, makes employees even more engaged and willing to work hard for the company, and enables us to lead with our values. A few years ago, we conducted an employment engagement survey. In 80 pages of comments, the most-used word was "family." That's partnership.

Customers

This is one of the most important aspects of this book, so much so that I've dedicated half of a forthcoming chapter to it. To be a successful company, one that truly leads from the front lines, you cannot simply view your customers as people to whom you sell. Rather, you must view your customers as partners that you work with to solve problems they have. This mindset shift opens a whole new range of possibilities for how your business operates, including empowering your employees to respond to new issues that your customers have.

To partner with your customers, you need to start with understanding them. What is their purpose? What are their competitors doing? What does the regulatory framework of their industry look like? What are their quarterly goals? Annual? What are the biggest challenges they are working to overcome? Once you know all of this, you can adjust your products and services in ways that best align with their priorities and the issues keeping them up at night. Maintain close contact with them, and align your product road map to grow in a way that is true to your purpose and theirs.

Suppliers

Just as you need to partner with your customers to be truly effective, you also need to partner with your suppliers. In the same way that you ask for feedback from your customers and try to understand their industries and their needs so you can innovate better solutions for them, you need to share your own needs and challenges with your suppliers. If your conversations with suppliers remain focused on contractual terms and standard performance expectations, then you're missing the opportunity to benefit from their knowledge and lessons learned. Seek to understand their purpose, mission, and values as well as their product and technology road maps (the planned improvements to products and technology within the organization). Check to see where they align with yours. See how they engage in developing their employees. How do they support their local community? See if you can find ways to combine efforts by cohosting shared events. Also, help them understand your end customer, so they can deliver innovative ideas and new solutions from their experience and collective knowledge, in the same way you would tap the brain trust of your teams.

If you don't find connections in any of those areas, then you may choose to continue working with that supplier based on strong quality or delivery performance. But you may do well to shop around and see if you can find a better partner that would provide greater opportunities to leverage outside resources to continuously innovate and remain competitive. In most large organizations, you get to evaluate and select new suppliers every week. Look at your sourcing processes, the request for proposal (RFP) forms, and how your organization identifies and considers new suppliers. Then build into those processes a few questions about suppliers' purpose and values, their long-term goals, and how they promote innovation, diversity, and inclusion. Choosing suppliers who align with your company's values in these areas will add a powerful new source of innovation and growth.

Another great way to embed shared purpose and innovation into the infrastructure of your company is to apply for certification with an external monitoring board, like the B Impact Assessment. This assessment, which more than 50,000 businesses have used, evaluates your company on its environmental impact, quality of governance (e.g., corporate transparency and accountability), community impact, and worker treatment. The process helps you examine each part of your company, including your supply chain, and identifies opportunities to build the governance processes, infrastructure, and decision-making framework to serve your purpose beyond just profits.

As we completed the survey for SUMMi7, it revealed we could improve how we fulfill our commitment to social and environmental responsibility, how we invest in our employees, and how we can better leverage and support local suppliers. As a result, we were able to incorporate repeatable processes that can help us be transparent about our purpose, measure our success living up to our commitments, and engage our employees, customers, and suppliers around common values and initiatives on which we can align our efforts to do better collectively. It also identified areas where we could select better partners to work with, so we not only walk the walk with our values but also find others who can bring diverse perspectives and innovative thinking to bear for our business.

Community Partners

Community partners are organizations, including state and local governments, nongovernmental organizations (NGOs), and other businesses, that may or may not be directly related to your industry and purpose, yet share your commitment to make an impact in the community. These partnerships tend to be less focused on the bottom line and are more about giving back to the community. Successful community partnerships are an invaluable way to help your company thrive while supporting the community at large. With community partners, you can demonstrate a genuine commitment to social good and open avenues to share expertise, all in service to solving more complicated problems than you could on your own.

This doesn't mean that you should indiscriminately pour money and labor hours into companies and NGOs. A partnership will only succeed when you can identify a shared interest between your group and the partners you seek. For example, as an aerospace company with our headquarters in Irving, Texas, Aviall partnered with the Irving Independent School District to support STEM (science, technology, engineering, and math) and aviation educational programs for teenagers. In doing so, we were able to connect one of our values (supporting education) with our company's need to develop talent for a future workforce, while we helped the school district better prepare students for careers in STEM.

Another basis upon which to form an effective partnership can be organizational values. Be aware that unless you cultivate an authentic connection between your company and another organization, your initiative might appear opportunistic. This can undermine trust between your organization and the community as well as breed resentment. Therefore, it's vital that both groups have a genuine shared interest in the partnership and strive to demonstrate a track record of dedication and commitment to the cause. At Aviall, we often formed partnerships with organizations that shared our dedication to service and our commitment to supporting veterans, which was a key part of our founder Edward Booth's motivation. To that end, we worked with many partners, such as the Adaptive Training Foundation, an organization that provides access and inclusion to disabled veterans to support wellness and create a community after their military service.

Industry Affiliates

This group is a bit broader and a bit more difficult to define. Generally speaking, industry affiliates are organizations or individuals that you partner with who help you achieve a specific business aim. They aren't necessarily suppliers or customers, or even organizations that primarily operate in the same industry as you do. Another way to think about this would be as a new network that can help you expand your perspective. The traditional view of networking is that you get to know people in the industry, and as you make connections, each new connection adds value to every other person already in the network. Today, when inter-industry collaboration is both more common and more necessary than ever, this same model applies, but multiplied to the nth degree. These are the people in your industry and adjacent to it that you invite to your platform, provided that you share a common thread *and* at least believe in their purpose.

Partnering with industry affiliates is a core part of our SUMMi7 strategy. Our purpose is to address social and economic inequalities, and we have collaborated with other companies and organizations that can help us expand our impact. Our partnerships fall into three main categories. The first is channel partners, which help us connect with the communities we serve. These partners include the Women's Business Enterprise National Council, a large network that provides support to and advocates for women-owned businesses, as well as several coworking spaces that rent to local businesses, local Chambers of Commerce, and other economic development organizations. We share elements of a common mission with each of these groups. They want to help their members succeed, and so do we, though our approaches may differ.

Second, we have resource partners, which include financial and professional services companies that provide resources to businesses, such as HR, IT, or legal support, or even entities that provide access to capital at fair rates. Through these partnerships, we can help the businesses going through our programs access whatever resources and guidance they need to scale successfully and with purpose.

Third, we cultivate a pool of what we call impact investors—large enterprises, either for-profit or NGOs, that share our mission and seek to promote economic development through direct, nonloan financial support. With these partners, we've developed a scholarship fund that allows underfunded or overstressed companies to invest in our programs.

These partnerships act as an impact multiplier for our organization. Not only do they help us provide a better service, they also allow us to reach new communities and to offer access to our service to people who otherwise would not have it.

The Next Level of Partnership: Building Global Coalitions

Coalition-building takes purpose and partnership and applies it at a the global level. As globalization accelerates, we increasingly face problems of existential significance. It's clear that the way we've been operating is unsustainable, and if we want life to continue on this planet in the long run, we need to create an unprecedented shift in the way that we lead *every single aspect* of our lives. Preserving our environment, combating climate change, reducing global poverty, fighting epidemics and pandemics—these sorts of problems require coalitions unified around a common purpose.

This level of leadership is both relatively new and vitally necessary in the modern age. To address these problems will require people from radically diverse backgrounds to work together, and stakeholders from hundreds of different countries and companies to truly see, listen to, understand, and empathize with one another. We will have to become comfortable navigating the difference in the values of how a company from India shows up versus a company from Germany. If we can't bridge those gaps in a respectful way—where everyone's voice is amplified in the process—then we won't be successful at building coalitions on this scale.

Ensuring that your company has strong, purpose-driven relationships with each of the six types of partners will provide the foundation for building these coalitions. Draw on your experience to create solutions that work for your company and all stakeholders; then apply that level of creative thinking to a global scale. Invite all of your partners to join you and to partner with and join each other. It's difficult, it may even seem impossible, but, to me, it's the ultimate goal of leadership.

3

PRACTICE RADICAL TRANSPARENCY

Microsoft cofounder Bill Gates famously said, "How you gather and manage information will determine whether you win or lose." He's right. Periods of rapid change demand rapid, intelligent decision-making. That is only possible if an organization can gather and share all the information it can. The easiest way to do that is to make information sharing uninhibited, which means practicing radical transparency, one of the most important aspects of frontline leadership.

Many managers and business leaders tout the necessity of transparency, and then take steps to implement policies that match what transparency means to them—like disclosing quarterly earnings or sharing memos on best practices. Other managers go a step further. Instead of merely explaining the company's performance and strategy, they also explain *why*. This second group of managers might think taking this extra step means that they are practicing radical transparency. For a long time, I was one of them. I believed that sharing the *what* and the *why* with my employees was enough.

But I was wrong. That just wasn't enough anymore because while employees could see what company leaders were thinking, *we couldn't see the employees or hear their points of view.* This was a major barrier. We hadn't created real transparency between the managers and executives and the rest of the organization. Instead, we'd hoisted a big screen and projected our image on it, but we couldn't see anyone who was watching. It doesn't matter how comprehensive or honest you are in your communications, if you haven't cultivated two-way communication, you aren't being fully transparent.

Radical transparency requires a dramatic departure from the old top-down leadership style, which assumes that only the most powerful members of an organization can be trusted with vital information and the ability to make decisions. This concentration of knowledge and power will lead to one of two things: either it slows decision-making because decisions must come from the top when most of the data comes from the bottom, or people on the ground will start making decisions without a view of the full picture, which, of course, will be uninformed and less effective. Either way, the top-down leadership style is less able to respond both to issues and opportunities, and will end up impeding a company's ability to compete, as other companies outmaneuver them. This is the new early mover advantage that younger companies have because companies generally start with a high level of transparency in their startup phase. They leverage that advantage to move into and take over markets that older companies have dominated for decades. This is the case with media, technology, retail, fashion, and numerous other industries that have been disrupted by newer, more agile startups. An often overlooked advantage is the radical transparency that enables rapid, continuous innovation on the front lines.

Contrary to that, when leaders in top-down organizations decide to give information to their employees, it's often in the form of orders, with little to no explanation as to why. These leaders act in a manner similar to how "lawn-mower parents" behave toward their children—cutting a prescriptive path to follow, which may be expedient in the short run, but denies children the opportunity to find solutions on their own and take ownership of their work. Such organizations become inflexible, as the slow flow of information precludes learning and adaptation, leading to greater costs and reduced relevance. In our rapidly changing world, these opaque organizations cannot survive.

Be Transparent with Yourself

A company will only go as far as its people can take it. This means that if you want your company to grow, inevitably, *you* must grow as well. No matter how much experience we may have, no living person is a finished product. If you want to take your organization to new heights, or even just keep up with the pace of change, you must constantly be learning more about yourself, identifying and leveraging your strengths, expanding your perspective to include that of others, and adapting to new challenges and opportunities.

Start by being transparent with yourself and work through the self-reflection described in Chapters 1 and 2. When you gain a clear understanding of your values and purpose, then you can incorporate that awareness into how you work with and lead others. Then get to know others' strengths and values, as well as how they work best, which will strengthen relationships and improve your ability to connect, communicate, resolve conflicts, and build trust in the workplace. This all helps set the stage for radical transparency.

Build this into a practice by evaluating feedback on how you lead, collaborate, and make decisions over time. Take a look at your actions over the last year and, to the best of your ability, evaluate what's working well and what's not. While this might be a challenge, recognize that the only way to learn from your mistakes is to admit them. You can only improve what you shine a light on and are comfortable talking about. We all have opportunities to improve. Recognizing them is part of the growth journey—not to be avoided but rather embraced as a way to lead by example.

Although understanding where we can improve is vital, we all also have strengths we can build upon that enable us to perform at our best. Make the effort to understand, acknowledge, and celebrate your strengths. If you only focus on weaknesses, you'll short-circuit your self-esteem and limit potential growth. I'm a big believer in strengths-based leadership that involves helping others identify and lead from a place of strength. We all may be a work in progress, but we also have natural abilities that we can develop, that energize us, and that we can use in service to a vocation.

For example, as I've said, I deeply value and have a natural orientation toward optimism. I cultivate it in myself, and I seek it out in other people. I'm also aware that in challenging situations, my optimism can disengage people, as it can give the impression that I'm being impractical or out of touch with what's happening. But by acknowledging my optimism up front and showing respect for other points of view, together, my team can tackle the reality of whatever problem we face.

Our strengths and imperfections are what make each of us unique. Going through the process of self reflection to understand our own opportunities to grow is what opens the door for transparency across an organization. This requires a willingness to be vulnerable with others.

Be Transparent with Your Teams

Vulnerability is a word that will come up over and over again in this chapter because radical transparency is impossible without it. We need to become comfortable being vulnerable. Just because you have figured out what you believe and what you value and how those impact your actions, doesn't mean that other people will suddenly understand it themselves. You have to show them.

When I returned to my role of CEO of Aviall, I held a town hall to reintroduce myself. I tend to be an introvert, but because I spoke from the heart and shared my excitement but also the wieght of the expectations that I now felt, I was able to be myself and felt more connected to my employees. They made it clear that they appreciated the honest, heartfelt conversation. Employees saw me as a vulnerable, multidimensional person, instead of a distant executive from headquarters. This helps bring a team together and it helped me get grounded. That first meeting energized me, and it set the tone for my tenure going forward. It established a baseline of trust and a commitment that we would share information freely, that we would create an environment in which everyone could speak with candor and authenticity, and that we would tackle challenges together. This expectation lay the foundation for us to reflect on our position, how we delivered value to our customers, and how we could improve. Together we were successful: Aviall's revenue and profit margin grew by more than 20 percent each year. Of course, it took more than a town hall meeting. We succeeded because of hard work and practicing the other principles of frontline leadership that followed, but it wouldn't have been possible without that baseline commitment to transparency, vulnerability, and teamwork.

Before that time, I didn't fully appreciate the need to share my thought process or my deeply held beliefs as part of my role as a leader. I often assumed that people already understood those, but people see things differently based on their own mindset, values, and experiences. When I led a meeting and just got straight to the point, side discussions followed, action slowed, and we would fall out of alignment—all because people didn't understand where we needed to go relative to where we were, and that included me. It wasn't until I started to take more time to go around the room to connect with each individual, to understand his or her assumptions and beliefs, and to work with each person to build a path forward, that we became efficient in making decisions and taking action. As the saying dictates, "Go slow to go fast." Invest the time up front to get aligned, or you'll spend more time down the road having to course correct.

Your commitment to vulnerability needs to be total, and a key facet of practicing that is striving to show up authentically in the office, just as you do at home. Many believe that to be an effective leader, you have to put on an act and behave like a "leader." Many people interpret that to mean that you have to have all the answers, put pressure on your employees, be decisive, and never allow dissent. It will be very difficult to build trust within an organization if you begin every meeting talking about the importance of transparency and inclusion and how those values guide our actions, only to turn around and make unilateral decisions without giving others a voice. Being vulnerable and radically transparent requires your actions to match your true values, instead of some image in your head of what a leader "should" be.

Not only will putting on an act degrade trust and effectiveness at work, it will also drain your energy. It is far harder to constantly monitor your behavior and try to make it align with an inauthentic ideal than to show up as your true self.

When I was younger, I thought I had to fit the mold of a manager in the office and then transition to dad and husband at home. It would take me a full hour to get that adjustment right! That was an hour of time and energy dedicated to shifting my role that I could have spent with my family. There will always be occasions when taking the time to transition is necessary—usually in moments of crisis, either at work or at home. You will need to maintain some boundaries, so that you don't let difficulty on the job bleed into and damage your home life. Yet, as much as you want to control your emotions and keep crises compartmentalized, there's nothing wrong with acknowledging that you are struggling with a difficult issue.

This is another part of vulnerability: the willingness to admit when you're not at 100 percent when there is something in your life or in your business that is throwing you off. Try as you might to hold it all together, if a crisis is big enough, it will impact the rest of your life. If you can own it and say to your employees, "Hey, I'm going through a difficult time; I've lost a member of my family," or however much you're willing to share, then your employees will know that you might not be as focused as always. They can be with you, offer support, and help pick up the workload. They can show they care about you and appreciate what you've done.

If as a leader you take the initiative to show vulnerability, including admitting when you're going through a tough time, that will go a long way toward creating a culture in which people feel comfortable showing vulnerability themselves and accepting whatever support they need. This enables people to make lasting and meaningful connections with their coworkers.

However, you can go beyond modeling behavior to build this type of culture. A great tool I've seen utilized to highlight the diversity of experience and perspective in the organization is to invite all employees to put together a one page that introduces them. They can include pictures from meaningful moments in their lives, and write a few bullet points about their biographies and personal values. We do a version of this in SUMMi7, and all our team members share and identify their underlying passions with their colleagues. Then, we toss aside traditional titles (e.g., chief operations officer, or COO) in an effort to make sure that we keep seeing the whole person, understanding personal motivations, and not just thinking about him or her in the context of a role or position.

Foster a Radically Transparent Culture

It's rare for people to achieve radical transparency on their own. It is much easier to do so within a strong culture of radical transparency—with people who help you be transparent. That's why, once you as a leader have made strides in being transparent with yourself, it becomes incumbent upon you to create the circumstances that will allow others to make the same breakthrough. Indeed, I wouldn't have developed this understanding of transparency if it weren't for one of my managers at Honeywell, Ron Utke. Ron embodied the vulnerability I discussed in the previous section—he was open and honest about his mistakes, he readily discussed emotions that arose around various problems, and he admitted when he didn't have all of the answers. He also was compassionate with himself and empathetic to others. He reflected on his choices and frequently shared those reflections with us. And he didn't just share aspects of himself with us, he also shared heaps of information about the company and talked through the thought process behind the decisions that he made.

I've always been a curious person and a "big picture" thinker, which has made me want to understand as much as I can about the larger puzzle and how all of the pieces fit together. My curiosity and Ron's openness were a natural match. I gravitated to him, asking endless questions about the company, my position in it, and how I could continue to grow and find new ways to contribute. We often spoke in the parking lot, late at night, hours after everyone else had gone home. He became a mentor, a friend, and someone who deeply impacted my approach to business in general and transparency in particular.

As my responsibilities as a young leader at Honeywell grew, I strove to emulate Ron's empathetic and vulnerable approach, while also sharing the sort of key information about the company that he had made available to me. Eventually, I got promoted and became a trained and certified Six Sigma Black Belt, an expert at breaking down processes and numbers to analyze and improve outcomes. This new certification, and the role that came with it, was perfect for a "big picture" thinker like me. It gave me a powerful toolkit that allowed me to dig into the details of how people and processes fit together to deliver outcomes, along with the ability to engage employees, lead change, and measure the impact of that change.

As part of that process of leading change, I would collaborate with working teams and diagram how what they did aligned with everything else going on in the organization. In this role, I started to develop my own practice of radical transparency. Here I had the opportunity to frame problems and document solutions while facilitating broad teams. I was encouraging them to share, to open up, to be transparent. From that point on, I've made continuous adjustments in my management and leadership style to draw out employees and make them feel as empowered as I did as a new hire at Honeywell.

At the start of this transformation, I viewed my job as identifying problems and finding solutions. Now, I strive for something completely different: I try to frame problems in a common language that empowers others who are closer to the problems to find the solutions themselves. In other words, it's my job to be radically transparent and foster frontline leadership. I feel like I've done my best work when I'm leading a meeting, writing down everything that's said on a whiteboard, at the end of which 95 percent of what I've written down was said by someone other than me—*and* everyone in the meeting has contributed.

To some outside observers, this might not look like success. It might not even look like work. All I did was organize, integrate, simplify, and frame the combined perspectives and shared learning from everyone in the room. My thoughts, decisions, and opinions were hardly heard, and maybe hardly made an impact, but I managed to connect everyone to a shared understanding. Despite appearances, this is no small feat. It takes active listening in meetings, years of consistent practice and self-reflection, and a concerted effort to build the right working environment in which people feel empowered *and* informed enough to offer their own ideas. It is much more difficult than just dominating a meeting, but it's also the best way to ensure inclusion and stoke innovation—which, often, can be the difference between evolving with the market or getting left behind.

This boils down to creating the right culture, one in which people trust you, are trusted themselves, and feel seen and heard. Everything we've talked about thus far will help you set the right tone. That said, there are certain practices that you can implement to encourage radical transparency. A great place to start—something you can do tomorrow—is to share more information with your employees. Walk through your profit and loss statement for last year with your team. Highlight the markets and customers that make up most of your business. Discuss the cost drivers and your margins by product line. Brainstorm actions that your team can take to better serve customers to drive top-line growth or lower costs to improve margins. Set stretch goals with a team incentive, so everyone shares in the success of the company. If done consistently, this combination of increased information and solicited input will help build trust in your company. And it will activate your employees as frontline leaders, emboldened to make proactive decisions. After taking that initial step, you can go deeper, by prioritizing four essential actions within the company:

- Listen to understand.
- Follow through to build trust.
- Establish clear expectations.
- Encourage proactive decision-making.

Listen to Understand

Radical transparency can help you build trust within your organization, but only if it's truly a two-way street. This makes intuitive sense: you can't build trust in any one direction if the other party doesn't reciprocate. In the normal course of operations at most businesses, there are countless opportunities to practice radical transparency by soliciting feedback from employees. Meetings present rich opportunities for this. If you, as a leader, start a meeting by honestly sharing where you are, where you want to go, and what the company's current struggles are, that's a great start. Then you can and should open up the floor to employees. Ask them what they've noticed that week, and encourage them to share any issues they've found or potential solutions or innovations.

Of course, there is a profound difference between *hearing* what employees say and actually listening to them and understanding their words in the context of your business and the challenges or opportunities you face. It's an inability to complete this last step that often prevents many well-meaning managers from practicing radical transparency. Effective communication is like a circle. After someone shares an idea with you, first check to make sure that you understood what was said, and encourage everyone else to do the same. Once you've confirmed that you understand, you can respond—and the cycle repeats.

As you gain insights from your team, you can start to recognize trends in how employees are engaging, collaborating, solving problems, and prioritizing their work. In other words, you can get a sense of how your culture is evolving. This gives you a chance to see if the elements of trust, open discussion, active engagement, shared responsibility, and collective efforts are working to support your company's goals and objectives. Engagement starts with listening and giving people a voice. Everything else flows from there.

One example of how this can be particularly powerful comes from one of our SUMMi7 strategy meetings. It was a five-person meeting over Zoom, during which I laid out a potential vision of what our online program and curriculum might be. It took me about 10 minutes, and I filled up three or four whiteboards with notes and diagrams. After the presentation, our marketing leader asked our creative director, "So, did you get all that?"

Our creative director hadn't caught everything, but he was still able to give a great summary in his own words. When he finished, I realized that he'd explained it better than I had. Listening to him helped me both understand and communicate my idea better. Our marketing leader then said, "Oh, I get it," and offered her own brief summary, which was slightly different from how I'd described it and what our creative director had said.

In the course of about 20 minutes, we'd all deepened our understanding of the idea. We'd each gained a 360-degree view of what we were talking about because we each approached it from our unique perspective and then *effectively shared* it. These are some of my favorite moments: when we are able to achieve this level of mutual understanding because it is often when real breakthroughs happen. People will be able to take their unique, deep understanding of the question at hand and innovate fresh ideas that create new opportunities. In sharing those with the group, they start off a whole new riff on the same idea. But none of this would be possible if we didn't first take the time to make sure everyone understood what we were talking about.

Follow Through to Build Trust

If your goal is to build trust within your organization, then you must extend your engagement with your employees' ideas beyond the meeting. For example, if, in a meeting, you solicit ideas or ask about potential problems, and an employee raises a hand and asks, "A lot of our customers are saying that their shipments are coming in late, even when we send them out on time. Are we doing anything to resolve that?"

If you just say, "Great point, thank you," and never bring it up again, you've missed the opportunity to build trust with that employee. You might have shown that you *heard*, but you failed to *respond*. Even if, after the meeting, you went and personally called the customer, figured out what the problem was, and resolved it, you still didn't practice radical transparency because you never completed the communication loop.

You must *always* follow through with your employees when they've shared something. If you don't, it can be even worse for your company than if you never solicited feedback in the first place. For an employee to bring up a process problem or offer an innovative idea requires that person to be vulnerable. The employee is raising an issue, which might cause conflict or even be admitting a personal failure. Or the employee is putting forward an idea, something that person might cherish and hold close to his or her self-esteem. If employees take that risk, only for their statements to be ignored or to disappear into the corporate ether, they will feel betrayed. If you consistently fail to complete the communication circle, you will reduce transparency because your employees will feel disrespected, leading them to build walls, conscious or unconscious, that stymie free-flowing communication.

There are many ways to close the communication circle. You don't need to give every employee an in-depth, on-the-spot answer, nor do you need to instantly go chase down a solution to every problem someone brings up—but you do need to do *something*. In smaller meetings, one-on-one settings, and with smaller issues or suggestions, the best course might be to offer a comprehensive answer in the moment, if you have one. If you don't have one, then admit that. One of the greatest mistakes that people can make is assuming they must always have all the answers. If you don't know something, own it, commit to get more information, and follow up with that employee once you get it. Or, if it's appropriate, delegate further exploration to the employee who brought up the issue or asked the question.

Returning to our previous example, if someone says, "Hey, customers are saying that shipments are coming in late even if we send them out on time. Are you looking into that?"

One of the best responses you as a leader can offer is something like, "Wow, great catch. Thank you for bringing that up. Can you find out more and recommend a solution? What can I do to help?" This is a chance to be authentic, reinforce the importance of empathy with your customers, and encourage employees that are closest to the problem to identify potential solutions.

This has a number of benefits. It encourages everyone in the room to start behaving like a frontline leader and to take more ownership over his or her work. The ultimate goal of the frontline leadership model is for you not to hear about a problem like that until the employee who noticed it had investigated it and maybe even tested a solution. By practicing this type of radical transparency, you can help employees develop the habit of recognizing and interrogating problems, and then looking for solutions on their own. Then, if they do run up against something that they cannot solve on their own, they will feel comfortable sharing it with you and have faith that if they do, you will respond to it because of the established pattern of effective communication.

Of course, sometimes what I just described is not possible. In my experience, when leading large meetings of more than 50 people, it's often best to focus on giving as many individuals a voice as possible, while I take notes. Then, at the end, I circle back, address everything that I can on the spot, and then tell people who have brought up more complicated issues that I will follow up with them within a reasonable timeframe. The last part of that statement is the most important. No matter what happens after you leave that meeting, no matter what you find out about the issue or what you decide, you have to follow up with whomever brought it up in the first place, even if the next steps do not directly impact that employee. If employees suggest a process tweak that you decide not to use, sit down with them and say that you appreciate the suggestion, but that you're going in a different direction and explain why. If they asked a question you didn't know the answer to, get the answer and then give it to them. Then you will have learned, and they will have learned. You'll have improved the flow of information through the company, and you will have fortified the expectation of honest, two-way communication. It doesn't have to be perfect, but you do have to show your authentic best effort and employees will appreciate that. If you don't have time to do all this work, it may be a sign that you're trying to take on too much or need to empower other leaders to engage as well.

Establish Clear Expectations

Radical transparency requires that you strive for clarity in all of your communications. Some of the most important communications revolve around expectations. If you have two teams, and one is waiting for work from the other before it can do its job, and the two teams don't have the same expectation about when and how the work will be done, there will almost always be conflict. These are the types of situations that cause major project delays, hurt feelings, and a general animosity between teams. It can bury your company.

One of my coaching clients, the owner and CEO of a custom sign manufacturing company, told me she was dealing with a lot of conflict among her various teams on the manufacturing end of the business. Because they make custom signs, there is no set standard on how each project will look. That means that the time it will take for printers, painters, designers, cutters, and others to do their part changes with each project. When they tried to make a standardized system (e.g., each sign will be designed within four days), it didn't work. Sometimes the sign would come in early, sometimes late, which made it extremely difficult to make accurate commitments to customers.

By digging deeper into her company's processes, she realized that the company couldn't set an expectation of service based on time. To figure out how to set the proper expectation, we went back to her purpose, and tried to find out how her unique capability allowed her to compete in the marketplace. We realized that, compared to her competitors, she placed a much higher value on creating quality signs and on flexibility in customization. She didn't care as much about the speed with which a sign was made, and she wasn't trying to make it at a low cost. Now she knows, when she's bidding on a project, that the signs she makes will take longer and may not be the lowest cost, but they will also be of higher quality and uniquely crafted.

Once she clarified her priorities, she collaborated with her team and challenged them to set their own expectations, their own standards of how the sign will look when they hand it off to the next link in the manufacturing chain. She told them to make these decisions in a way that prioritized quality and flexibility.

This approach is radically different than the manufacturing model popularized by Ford and emulated for decades. In Ford's model, you had a supervisor standing behind you with a stopwatch, telling you to finish a part within a certain timeframe and send it along. That top-down model can have disastrous consequences in today's environment, including lower quality or robbing employees of any sense of ownership over their work. They aren't doing it on their terms, to their standards, or to their rhythms. In the long run, this can hurt you more than it helps.

Once expectations were in place, she installed a system to track it all. In this case, all of her teams work at the same site, so she was able to put a big monitor on the wall that showed the progress of each project. That way, any given team could look up and know when it could expect to get the next sign that needed cutting or painting or whatever stage was within the team's domain. Once the team receives it, if the sign has a quality issue or is incomplete, they know they can send the sign back to the other team with the note, without having to get the CEO involved. This is radical transparency in action—people communicating what they expect and what they are doing at any given moment. No ball is dropped because everybody knows who's responsible for which ball and when.

Encourage Proactive Decision-Making

When transparent two-way communication with clear expectations becomes the norm, it enables frontline leadership and strengthens the organization. One of the risks of having more moving parts and more decision makers is that a decentralized power structure can increase the odds of miscommunication. With this, you risk some degree of operational redundancy—of having someone start an initiative that appears to encroach on someone else's territory, or having two teams test new solutions in ways that aren't aligned. While a strong shared sense of purpose and aligned goals within the company can do a lot to mitigate these risks, the regular practice of two-way communication and radical transparency will go a long way toward ensuring that these issues, if they occur, can be quickly resolved.

Use radical transparency to train people to grow into the role of a frontline leader and to make them feel connected to the whole of the company. A great way to do that is to involve your employees in the decision-making process. Instead of a small group of executives developing a strategy and sending out the actions, include your frontline employees in the strategy creation process. Often, they will have the most up-to-date information about the operations of the business, the challenges in meeting goals, or changing customers' needs. Open a dialogue with them as part of the process to understand the strategic issues and opportunities facing the company and get feedback on potential decisions to be made as well as the supporting tactics to meet your long-term objectives. There's almost always more than one way to accomplish a goal, and more often than not, the solution is the one that your employees buy into the most.

That said, you still have information that they don't necessarily have access to, which you must share with them. When you ask people to give feedback on the company's annual, 5-year, or 10-year plan, they won't be able to engage with you unless they understand how you came to that decision. Ultimately, the question isn't whether the *plan* is right, but what does the plan *assume* is right? What assumptions—about the progress of the company, the shifts in the market, the changes in regulations—are you making? Of course, any sort of long-term projections can be thrown way off by one singular event (e.g., COVID-19), but that doesn't mean that you can't ever predict what the environment will be like a couple of years down the road.

Your strategy, then, is an anticipatory response to what you think will be happening. The more accurate your assumptions and your projections, the better your decisions will be that position your company for growth. If your employees already understand your assumptions when offering feedback on a new strategy and maybe even challenge your assumptions with information from their own experience talking to customers or competitors, then you can have productive debates that will propel the company forward.

This, again, requires vulnerability—especially from leaders. You must start from the realization that you do not have all the answers, and hold a genuine desire not only to listen to other perspectives but integrate them into the plan. This requires you to *examine* all of the assumptions that underlie your decisions before you share them. Whether or not we realize it, most of us make decisions based on deeply held beliefs and predilections (e.g., for or against risk).

Even if it doesn't spur debate right away, understanding and sharing these assumptions will pay huge dividends down the road. All strategies, even the best ones, need to change. Sometimes a small shift in buyer preference or in oil prices or even the weather will change the outlook for your business and render your assumptions inaccurate. Sometimes a much broader issue, like a pandemic, knocks you off course. Either way, you will need to develop on-the-fly responses—this is what "agility" means for a company. If your frontline employees understand the goals that drive your strategy, as well as the assumptions behind it, then when an inevitable event arises that requires a strategic tweak, they can make that change themselves. They don't need to wait through three cycles of business performance reviews for it to bubble up to the senior leadership team, only for the team to finally realize that one of its assumptions was off.

Practice Radical Transparency with Customers

The final part of radical transparency extends beyond your organization and incorporates your customers and community members. Few organizations do this better than the clothing brand Patagonia. Its mission is to "Build the best products, cause no unnecessary harm, use business to inspire and implement solutions to the environmental crisis," and its values are transparency, collaboration, and improvement.

Patagonia backs up all of this talk with nearly unprecedented transparency about where its products come from, its manufacturing practices, and the overall environmental and social impact of its products. Because of this transparency, customers know what they're buying, employees know how they contribute to a higher purpose, and the company is able to inspire extremely high levels of engagement with those who share its values and purpose.

But radical transparency with your customers and community stakeholders, just like radical transparency within your organization, needs to be a two-way street. You need to enter into true, trusting partnership with your customers, and you have to encourage their feedback and let it guide your own activities, as long as those activities are aligned with your purpose. Sometimes, that can mean making difficult decisions, and here again Patagonia serves as a powerful example. In keeping with its purpose, Patagonia regularly partners with environmental groups and other for-profit companies that prioritize sustainability.

For years, Patagonia had cobranding partnerships with many Wall Street banks and finance firms. At a certain point, it made the decision, informed by the environmental groups the company partnered with, that many of those finance firms actively undermined and contributed to the degradation of the environment. So in 2019, Patagonia stopped entering into cobranding partnerships with them, and instead sought cobranding opportunities with environmental groups, outdoor sports brands, and other transparent organizations that have a consistent, authentic commitment to protecting the environment. This is true transparency—listening to your stakeholders, integrating their feedback, and moving together toward a common purpose.

Self-Compassion Enables Transparency

While we all can and should strive to do and be the best that we can in any given circumstance, it's important to recognize that you're enough—even before you achieve a goal and even if you don't succeed. A failure to take this compassionate approach with yourself will not only make you miserable, it will reduce your effectiveness as a leader and prevent you from exhibiting one of the most important traits of radical transparency: empathy. Because radical transparency requires two-way communication, you need to be able to understand the feelings and thoughts that drive what employees say and how they act.

If you believe that you have to prove you're enough by reaching a very high standard, that means that you believe the same about everyone around you. And it's impossible to empathize with your employees if you can't demonstrate compassion with yourself. Some of the most ambitious people might scoff at this. We have an image of a leader, very much popularized in the "greed-is-good" 1980s and 1990s, as someone who is successful *because* he or she lacks empathy. The person is cutthroat, able to outperform competitors, rise to the top of the firm, and seize the market. Empathy, in that model, is a sign of weakness.

None of this is true. Excellence and empathy can coexist, and if you want your organization to rely on frontline leadership and be truly sustainable and healthy, then excellence and empathy *must* coexist. Recognize that you will trip, and so will everyone else. This is natural. What's most important is for you to help your employees get back up and continue to grow—and you can only do that with empathy.

SHOW THAT YOU CARE

4

The importance of showing that you care hit home for me in the Human Resources office at Honeywell. It was my first leadership job, and I was struggling with an employee problem, so I sought HR's guidance. During our meeting, the HR leader was sitting behind her desk, typing with her head down. The entire time, she never stopped typing, never moved from her desk, never even *looked* at me. It gave me the impression that she didn't care one bit about what I had to say. I felt stranded and alone, and wondered how much the company cared about me or my team. Fortunately, that was the exception, and I found plenty of support through other leaders.

However, I never forgot how that degree of indifference felt. I imagined what it would be like to work in a place where my boss and all of my peers treated me with the same coldness. Would I be happy in my job? Would I care about the company? Would I believe in its purpose or that it cared about helping its customers, if it didn't even seem to care about me?

On that day, I vowed to never make an employee feel the way I'd felt. This commitment to a culture of caring has proven invaluable. First of all, a caring culture helps establish trust between leaders and employees. Employees know that leaders make decisions with employees' success in mind, not just their own. Second, it helps employees feel confident and willing to engage in open dialogue with management. They offer input freely, and when they don't understand an initiative or direction, they feel comfortable enough to ask for clarification or recommend alternatives. Beyond that, when employees know that their supervisors and the company care about them and their well-being, they, in turn, care more about the company and offer greater support to their colleagues and peers. They put in the discretionary effort, and make proactive decisions that help drive the whole company forward. They behave like frontline leaders.

While caring for everyone matters, one area in particular requires extra effort: inclusion. Most companies hire people who fit with their culture, and new hires who don't often struggle. Over time, this encourages cliques to develop, which raises costs and saps productivity. Hiring only one type of person with the same worldview as everyone else is even worse. When companies do that, culture calcifies and stagnation takes hold.

This can seem like a double-bind: hiring diversely can create division, while hiring a group of facsimiles kills innovation. The path out of this bind is to create an open, caring culture that welcomes and celebrates differences.

Create a Caring Culture

Leaders set the culture of a workplace, so to create a culture of caring, you've got to model it. This is particularly important when you're a new leader taking over a team. The first six months set the tone of the manager–employee relationship, and modeling caring and empathy at the beginning will go a long way toward fostering a caring culture. Also, in those early days, new leaders know the least about their roles, so, to get up to speed, you'll need to rely on your team members. Reach out to each and every individual and start to foster a personal connection. Once you've done that, you can begin holding your team up to its own standards and values.

Empathy and caring are so personal in nature that they can be hard qualities to describe and almost impossible to teach. That said, I have three principles that have helped me establish a culture of caring in several environments throughout my career:

- Get to know people on their own terms.
- Value people over performance.
- Serve others, invest in their success.

Get to Know People on Their Own Terms

When I'm in a new leadership position, and I want to meet with all of my employees, instead of summoning them to my office, I walk to theirs. This small, simple gesture can go a long way toward showing that you value and respect your employees' time, and you're willing to go to where they feel most comfortable to speak. For example, at Aviall, when I managed a group of workers at an off-site distribution center, I would make weekly visits to the center to talk *with* (not *to*) the employees, shoulder to shoulder, on the floor of their work area.

The point of this pattern of engagement is to be actively listening. Don't just have a conversation and try to plan what you will say next. Listen to understand, and incorporate the feedback into your perspective. And, as discussed in the previous chapter, always be sure to follow up on a conversation with action.

Not every conversation will focus on business operations. In companies with strong cultures of caring, and if you're successful as an empathetic leader, then your employees might open up about personal struggles in their lives. For these conversations, active listening still reigns supreme, but following up with an action isn't always appropriate. Often, people just need to talk. In those cases, a response like, "You have my confidence and an open invitation to discuss further, and I will not share this with anyone else," is the most powerful thing you can offer.

Sometimes, an employee might bring up a personal issue that does require action. In those cases, I offer to help, unless I don't feel qualified to assist, in which case I'll ask something like, "Do you mind if I share that with our HR team members, so that they can support you in this area?" Obviously, don't coerce someone into taking your help or share their struggles with people they might not trust. Often, just knowing that help exists and that people care provides comfort.

While it is important to be available, you can overdo it. Too frequent drop-ins interrupt productivity and make employees feel coddled. Worse, it becomes disruptive to doing your job. That's why it's vital that you set manageable expectations around availability. As long as you're transparent and consistent about how much support you can offer, people will understand. For example, after working in distribution for Aviall, I had a brief stint with another business. A bit later, I returned to Aviall, this time as the CEO. I no longer had the time to visit the distribution center every week, so instead I went every month. Nobody ever complained about how little he or she saw me. Instead, every time I made a visit, an employee would say some version of, "Hey, Eric, thank you for still coming out, even though we aren't your direct reports. We love to see you and have a chance to share our perspectives."

This last anecdote illustrates another important point: your commitment to care shouldn't change with your circumstances. Nowhere is this truer than when something happens that requires big, difficult decisions, such as the coronavirus pandemic. As a member of the aviation industry, I saw first-hand the disruption that a decrease in air travel caused, and witnessed as several companies handled the crisis with empathy and grace. One company that stood out was Southwest Airlines, which has a well-earned and longstanding reputation as one of the most caring aviation companies. Through the start of 2021, Southwest had managed to avoid any furloughs or layoffs, even while its competitors resorted to furloughing off tens of thousands of employees.[*]

Southwest was able to do this, in part, due to its long track record of success. It has turned a profit in 47 of its past 50 years by building an entire brand around caring for the customer more than the bottom line. Its consistent profitability left it in a comparably strong position in the face of a dramatic decline in air travel. Beyond that, the company did everything it could to maintain its full workforce. It started at the top, when their CEO, Gary Kelly, decided to forgo his salary. Because he showed his own willingness to sacrifice for the good of the company and for the good of his employees, he could then ask other people, including top executives, to take a 10 percent pay cut. As the pandemic worsened and air travel fell further, Southwest offered voluntary leaves of absence and early retirement packages to some employees. It all worked. The company navigated the

---

[*] Associate Press, "Southwest Airlines lifts threat of furloughs after relief bill signed," KTLA, December 28, 2020, https://ktla.com/news/nationworld/southwest-airlines-lifts-threat-of-furloughs-after-relief-bill-signed/.

pandemic without resorting to furloughs or layoffs, and showed each employee just how much it really did care.*

Value People Over Performance

People *always* come before performance because it's your people who make performance happen. Not all companies see it this way. This, at least in part, explains why we see such poor engagement among US employees across all industries.

If you truly take care about your people, the performance will come. I first felt the power of this while leading the supply chain at L3 Vertex, a division of L3 Communications. My wife, Shelby, and I had moved from Portland, Oregon, to Madison, Mississippi, for that job. It was a bit of a culture shock at first, but it turned out to be the strongest community I've ever experienced, with a leadership team to match. People looked out for each other at work and at home, connected personally and professionally, and truly cared for one another, the company, and our customers.

I was fortunate to have that community. A couple years later, L3 transferred me to Greenville, Texas. During that time, we had our first son, Koen. Being a new parent is always hard, but we faced a unique challenge: Koen was born with clubfoot. In his first two months of life, he had to have surgery, wear seven casts during a seven-week period while he healed, and don leg braces 18 hours a day for two years, just to ensure he'd be able to walk correctly. It was a traumatic time, full of uncertainty and pain. No parents should have to force a cast onto their screaming infant once, much less once a week. Today, Koen is doing

---

* Glen Hunter, "Will Southwest Airlines Lose That Lovin' Feelin'?," *Texas Monthly*, October 30, 2020, https://www.texasmonthly.com/news/southwest-airlines-covid-pandemic-changes/.

great, plays football and lacrosse, and is one of the fastest kids on the team.

We got through it in no small part because of the community that existed within our company. I felt free to share my struggles with my colleagues, and they came to our home and dropped off casseroles and other meals for my wife and me, leaving signs with encouraging words on our door, and even taking on a little of my workload around the office. When things stabilized at home, I felt an immense connection to the company, to my peers, and to my friends, and I threw myself into my work with even more zeal. I vowed to lend the same level of support to my colleagues and employees, whenever and wherever it was needed.

Unfortunately, I didn't have to wait long to make good on this vow. A short time after, the most devastating thing imaginable happened to one of my team leaders: he lost his son in a car accident. I knew, as did his other colleagues, that the only thing that mattered was supporting him the best we could. Sometimes that meant providing flexibility at work or jumping in to help get things done. Other times it meant sitting silently on his back porch and just being there, present with him and his family.

The beautiful thing about these connections is that they last. Even when someone leaves the company, you've created a bond with that person, a real relationship, that will extend into the future. That person and every person in the company will become a part of your support system as you move through the rest of your life. I felt this after I left L3, and my wife and I lost our second child during the second trimester of her pregnancy. The leader I worked for at Aviall understood and offered his support throughout this trying time. But even if he hadn't, I know we would have made it through because when the people we'd known in Mississippi heard about what happened, *they* reached out to us as well.

It is this sort of support that keeps people resilient, that allows them to weather the challenges of life and come back more powerful, more committed, and more dedicated to the purpose of the company than ever.

Serve Others—Invest in Their Success

Whenever I start to feel disconnected from my purpose, I ask myself: "What can I do to serve someone else today?" Then I just go and do it. The joy that comes from finding one or two people to help without asking anything in return almost always pulls me out my funk and reminds me why I do what I do.

One of the best ways to serve others is to invest in their success. Nobody achieves success without huge amounts of support along the way. My own history is full of mentors and colleagues whose help pushed me to the next level. But one person made a crucial, early investment in my success that made a huge difference in my career: Professor Jean Wilberg, who taught my calculus class during my freshman year in college.

I come from a working-class family, and was the first to graduate from college. Despite having worked and saved since the age of 12, sometimes working three jobs at once, we couldn't afford a private college. Instead, I started at SUNY Morrisville, a two-year school, in its engineering transfer program that would allow me to finish my four-year degree at a different institution. After all of that work, I almost derailed during my first semester. I came down with mononucleosis and strep throat at the same time. My throat was so swollen I couldn't eat, and I landed in the hospital for a week. While there, Professor Wilberg sent me class notes and assignments, so I could try to keep up with my studies.

When I returned to class, still suffering the lingering fatigue from mono, I found it impossible to stay awake. It didn't help that her calculus class was at 8 a.m. every day. Even though I'd always enjoyed math, I couldn't keep my eyes open through the whole class. Professor Wilberg provided flexibility on my assignments and tutored me during office hours and outside of class. Knowing that she cared about me and supported my success helped me find the energy to persist, when I very well may not have made it through. I owe a great deal of my success to Professor Wilberg. It helped me to recognize that not everyone has this sort of support network, so it's best to provide it to others when you can.

Investing in the success of your employees goes beyond helping them through adversity. If one of your employees is reaching for a goal, looking for new training or new opportunities, lend your help. Pay forward the help that your received to get where you are. When you invest in your employees and they grow, your company will grow with them.

Look Beyond Diversity to Inclusion

Many business leaders talk about the value of diversity, claiming that they view the individual differences between their employees as a source of tremendous strength. These same leaders might even back it up by broadening their recruitment strategies, looking beyond top MBA programs for job candidates, seeking hires from other industries, and/or prioritizing minority applicants. But then, their business doesn't actually improve. Sometimes things get worse, and the diverse team members whom they worked so hard to recruit leave. When this happens, it's because diversity alone is not enough.

Inclusion is when you combine diversity with caring, and it's far more powerful. Whereas diversity is measured in numbers (e.g., "We have 15 Black, 9 Hispanic, and 3 Asian employees."), inclusion is measured by how those employees *feel* in the work environment. To measure inclusion, you need to go beyond the hard statistical data and consider your team through the lens of empathy. Pay attention, work to understand how employees feel, find out whether they're uncomfortable in the workplace and in what ways. This requires a lot more effort than looking at the demographic breakdown of the company, but the added effort pays off. This sort of empathy unlocks the strength that true inclusion can provide.

In cases where empathy is absent, the tunnel-vision focus on diversity at the expense of inclusion prevents employees from demonstrating two key behaviors: engagement and authenticity.

If employees from an underrepresented background don't feel included and cared for, then they will never buy into the company enough to *engage* fully in their roles. They will feel like outsiders within their own organization, and from this orientation, they won't connect to the company's purpose. This level of disengagement can lead to devastating results. Employees who feel like outsiders will rarely exert any sort of discretionary effort. They will do the bare minimum instead. They will hang back in meetings, preferring to stay on the bench instead of jumping in to participate.

Feeling like an outsider also often prevents employees from showing up as their full, authentic selves. Each individual's unique perspective is the source of his or her best contributions to the workplace and the strength that increased diversity offers. However, if a company hires from diverse backgrounds, and a manager shoots down the first couple of ideas that a new employee offers with a dismissive, "That's not how we do things here," then that act will have negated the benefit of adding diversity.

Most employees will respond to that kind of hostility by trying to assimilate. In doing so, the employee learns to think in accordance with the company culture, obliterating personal perspective in the process. This creates a major problem: even if that employee is engaged and giving full effort, he or she won't bring the full weight of personal uniqueness and creativity to bear on a problem, making it unlikely that employee will contribute a revolutionary idea. Once this happens, even as the company brings in new talent, it simultaneously stifles innovation, which inevitably will lead to decreased competitiveness and lost market share. On the other hand, if you can create an inclusive environment, where your employees feel *authentically engaged* in their work, you will gain a huge competitive advantage.

Having a strong culture of caring will go a long way toward fostering inclusion, but there are three specific tactics to bring everyone onto the playing field:

- Promote edge players to build bridges across silos.
- Value all viewpoints.
- Meet people where they are.

Promote Edge Players

When I see a company struggle with interoffice communication, one of the first things I ask is, "What are the silos?" What I'm asking is where are the barriers between sectors or departments that keep them from sharing information? Usually, these toxic "in" and "out" cliques are responsible when a company struggles with internal communication. Communication breakdowns cause a whole host of problems, including costly infighting, a lack of innovation, and reduced engagement from any employees, teams, or departments that believe they are part of the "out" group.

The solution to this is to get the silos to start communicating again. One of the best ways to do that is to find and promote edge players. An edge player is someone with the necessary expertise to understand two distinct fields within the business—for example, operations and finance—and play in both. People who specialize in those separate fields not only perform different functions, they tend to speak different business languages. The operations side focuses on serving the customer, whereas in finance, everything often revolves around numbers and spreadsheets. In certain organizations, members of one team, say, operations, might feel more valued by upper management, and therefore, behave arrogantly and demean or minimize the contributions of the finance group, or vice versa. In reality, these are just two sides of the same coin, and both teams are trying to do what's best for the company. But neither can do that if they don't communicate.

An example of an edge player would be someone who understands a balance sheet and working capital. This person can explain to the finance team the importance of investing in people, while helping the operations folks see how handling (or mishandling) inventory impacts the bottom line.

Seek out the people in your organization who have the experience to help build these bridges, and then position them to do so. Give them more responsibility, and ask them to start sharing their knowledge with their colleagues. If each team is led by an edge player, then you will quickly sew up the gaps in your organization. These leaders will help divergent teams find common ground on which they can build the trust necessary to create a more productive working environment. If your organization doesn't have a lot of edge players on staff already, then make a conscious effort to hire and develop more. The next time you need to hire someone for your supply chain, look for someone with deep knowledge in IT, so that person can start to work on and think about how your information technology interacts with the supply chain. Workers with this sort of diversified background not only help build effective communication, they often innovate on their own. Better yet, begin a program to develop edge players internally by structuring rotations for employees through different departments. This allows them to gain new skills and perspectives, and bring those together as they grow with your company.

Value All Viewpoints

To build an inclusive organization, leaders need to expand their view of what constitutes a contribution. An organization that succeeds in recruiting a diverse workforce will have access to a range of opinions about how best to solve a problem, but only if leaders are able to draw these thoughts out and know how to leverage this variety of opinions.

Often, new employees have a tendency to hang back in meetings, believing that they need to get the lay of the land before contributing. This is natural, as people tend to develop a sense of psychological security at their own rate. But leadership can accelerate this process by establishing a culture of caring and openness that invites new employees to join the conversation. Management can and should go a step further to engage new employees and get their perspectives, starting out one-on-one in a safe environment, and then encouraging them to share their views in groups.

Often, people stuck in the day-to-day of company operations become blind to glaring inefficiencies. Each time a new pair of eyes enters the ecosystem, you have an opportunity to remedy that. Make sure that everyone shares and contributes—new and established, naturally loquacious and quiet. Leave no one out. Listen. Synthesize. Encourage respectful disagreement. This is how you can begin to leverage diversity.

Meet People Where They Are

In any discussion about diversity and inclusion, we must pay special attention to historically disadvantaged groups. It is easy to feel like an outsider if you are the only Black employee in a company, or the only Asian American, the only immigrant, or the only disabled person in an office. It is incumbent on you, as a leader, whatever your background, to meet people where they are, as they are, by creating an environment that genuinely values and cares for people of every background.

Creating such an environment can have massive benefits for your business. Many of the most talented people come from diverse and disadvantaged backgrounds. Often, those who faced adversity growing up had to develop grit to overcome those challenges and become the most successful executives. Even though it's been proven again and again that overcoming challenges fosters the greatest contributors, we as a society still hold unconscious biases against people who probably deserve our admiration. Both in society and at work, we often fail to amplify these voices. But if we are going to break down barriers and leverage all the talent that our communities, our country, and the world have to offer, we have to expand our view of "qualified," respect the different career journeys that people have, and recognize the unique strengths they bring. As I heard one well-respected leader say, "If it's not painful, if we're not breaking a process, then we're not trying hard enough and taking the actions needed for change."

For some employees, like the differently abled, the physical environment of the workplace can present a barrier to inclusion. Be mindful to equip all workspaces to be accessible to all of your workers. And, if and when you discover a barrier to engagement, remedy it as quickly as possible.

For example, during the coronavirus pandemic, a colleague told me a story about how, when her manufacturing plants reopened, one of her shift supervisors noticed a problem. One of her employees who had hearing loss relied on lip reading to communicate with her colleagues, but the masks people were wearing made that impossible. That same day, the supervisor placed a large order for face masks with clear plastic windows over the mouth area, so that all of her teammates' mouths would be visible. This is one of my favorite stories because it demonstrates two things that often go hand in hand: frontline leadership and a culture of caring. Because the supervisor cared about the employees' safety and ability to communicate and she was empowered as a frontline leader, she proactively got them the equipment they needed so that they could stay safe and effective.

Once you've created an inclusive physical environment, you can focus on creating an inclusive atmosphere as well. This requires the cultivation of a deep, reflective empathy. Like every sort of empathy, this is deeply personal, and most people will have to figure it out on their own. There are two things that will help everyone on this journey: listening and striving to see the entire person. From my perspective as a white male, when those from a disadvantaged community share their experiences, I listen to them, respecting what they say but acknowledging that I may never fully understand. And then I commit to continue listening, sharing perspectives, and slowly bringing them together over time. Inclusion takes long-term commitment, with progress made in small interactions and intentional effort.

Part of the reason that I started SUMMi7 was to provide education and coaching to minority-, women-, and veteran-owned small businesses. The fact is, because of structural barriers that have existed for the entire history of the United States, if you're a Black entrepreneur, odds are you have had less access to mentorship, education, business owner networks, startup funding, and loans. If we truly want to live up to our stated ideals, we need to invest in our minority communities, build up Black-owned businesses that can help create more leaders as role models who can, in turn, reinvest in schools and communities. All of us need to advocate for and provide more resources to communities that haven't received the same level of support.

At SUMMi7, it is our belief that we can do our part by building a movement. Our goal is to enable economic equity, promote diversity and inclusion, and embed social responsibility into how businesses are run. One way this manifests is going into underserved communities to listen, so that we can better understand the unique needs and challenges that businesses face. Four out of the five businesses in our first pilot cohort were minority-owned. Everyone matters, everyone's success matters, but certain groups face greater barriers to success, and we must acknowledge that disparity and do what we can to remedy it. My team and I discussed how quickly we can get another cohort up and running focused on Black-owned businesses.

There are movements underway around the world that support racial equity and justice. The world is watching as we try to find ways to address the underlying problems that have led us to where we are today. Inspired by this, after 10 years at Boeing, I transitioned to pursue my purpose with the SUMMi7 team full time, during what I consider to be a critical turning point in our history as a society.

5

MAINTAIN ALIGNMENT THROUGH CHANGE

Every company either adapts to the changing environment or moves a little closer to its demise. The numbers are jarring. Most small businesses don't survive past the first five years. Larger companies fare better, but even they can fall precipitously, from thriving to extinct in one year. This is especially true in the twenty-first century, when technological change brings the constant risk of disruption from new, more nimble competitors. Large companies that intend to stick around can't just double down on what they've always done. They cannot merely react to the change; they must begin to lead it.

This poses a challenge: ideas that redefine an industry tend to come from younger, smaller companies, with the agility to outflank established market leaders. Large companies can counter this by embracing frontline leadership and empowering all employees to make the small changes that add up to large-scale innovation. Taking this on carries a significant risk: if everyone tries out his or her own solutions, it might pull the company in a thousand different directions. To prevent this, a company needs to actively maintain alignment, making sure that each member of the organization moves in the same direction.

The ability to maintain alignment in the face of constant change requires two objectives all employees must embrace:

- Everyone must operate in service of the company's purpose.
- They must foster frequent and clear communication across teams.

Putting in place structures to support these objectives will allow you to take advantage of the changing landscape.

Operate in Service of the Company's Purpose

The most important part about maintaining alignment with a frontline leadership system is to make sure that everyone connects to the company's purpose and understands its core values. Take time to underscore how every decision aligns with the company's purpose, values, and beliefs. Before you commit to any change initiative, be sure the "how" aligns with your core values and the "why" moves the company closer to its purpose. Reinforce this connection every day. That way, you create an environment where empowered employees will make decisions that align with the company's purpose and implement them in a way that reinforces your values and culture. Only then can you rest assured that it is a beneficial change.

Knowing your initiative is aligned with your purpose is only the first step. It's essential that the company *practices* its purpose on a day-to-day basis. For example, a nonprofit that invests heavily in the aesthetics of its brand fails to demonstrate consistent alignment to its purpose and values, as its choices prioritize optics (e.g., extravagant offices) over legitimate change and impact. This creates a dissonance in the organization and could lead employees to do the same by, say, looking productive but not getting much done. Compounded, these dissonant choices will pull the organization out of alignment.

Foster Frequent and Clear Communication Across Teams

To leverage change, a company must be aligned with both its purpose and the objectives that are cascaded down to each team. In times of flux, people need to have a clear grasp of the goals, expectations, responsibilities, and actions of every other team. This involves the radical transparency I described earlier—where everyone should know as much as possible about the financial status of the company and the overall shape of the market, so that each employee has context about where the company stands. But transparency only gets you so far. You also need to foster frequent and clear communication between and across teams. This winning combination empowers employees to make informed decisions on their own. In a sense, your degree of alignment depends on how committed to radical transparency you are. The more that your business and the world around it is changing, the more transparency you'll need. This is especially true if you're trying to implement some sort of innovation. As Muriel Strode said, "I will not follow where the path may lead, but I will go where there is no path, and I will leave a trail."*

---

* Susan Ratcliffe, ed., *Oxford Essential Quotations*. (Oxford: Oxford University Press, 2017), online version accessed May 18, 2021, https://www.oxfordreference.com/view /10.1093/acref/9780191843730.001.0001/q-oro-ed5-00019835.

The trail is the most important part of this. An innovation will only succeed if everyone contributes to the discovery. Transparency and consistent, clear communication about all of the metrics helps everyone get on the path. It fosters inclusion, so you can bring the whole team on the trail, and gain the benefit of each member's specific knowledge as you discover the unknown.

I've found three keys to creating that trail:

- Connecting the organization
- Conducting visual meetings
- Creating project-specific waypoints to guide progress

Connect the Organization

For an organization to maintain alignment, everyone needs to understand his or her individual goals within the context of the organization's goals and purpose. A great tool to transmit this information is a Goal Deployment Matrix.

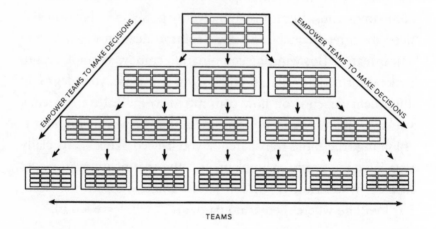

In this matrix, you break down the organization into levels of leadership. Each level has a scorecard that measures key performance indicators (KPIs), which differ according to the specific team. For example, when I was CEO of Aviall, my leadership team and I met each week to review our performance in sales, customer feedback, and on-time delivery ratings. Then all members of my executive management team would go over their scorecards with their respective teams to evaluate their own performance. The vice president of operations had an operational scorecard, the vice president of sales and marketing had a sales and marketing scorecard, and the CFO had a financial scorecard that included the income statement, cash flow, and so on.

We then broke that down further. Within operations, there was a planning team, a distribution team, and a procurement team, each with its own specialized scorecard. Then we broke it down yet again. Each warehouse had a shipping team and a receiving team with separate scorecards, and so on, across each team at each level of the company.

Each day, I would see the aggregated performance of each team in relation to its goals. I could then reference these hyperspecific metrics in any meetings with employees from different levels and at companywide town halls. When I said to the whole company, "Our on-time delivery goal was 99 percent of our orders, but last month we only got to 98 percent," everyone in the meeting connected to that. They had their team's scorecard, and they knew whether they hit 99 percent on-time delivery or they only reached 95 percent. If they hit 95 percent, they knew they had opportunities to improve and could reach out to other teams for support. They reflected on their performance and held themselves accountable, without leaders having to take punitive action. Companies that rely on punitive actions rarely improve actual performance. Instead, they train employees to avoid scrutiny and punishment by gaming the metrics. Problems don't disappear, they fester. It's far better to recognize that, at some point, everyone will have a day when goals are not met. What's most important is to support all the teams, not punish them.

Of course, they will only put in that extra effort to hold themselves accountable if they feel connected to the company's purpose. In the abstract, these metrics mean almost nothing to most frontline employees, but they are an essential part of fulfilling a company's purpose. The greatest limit on a company's impact is its size, resources, and profits, so you need to connect these to the company's purpose. Help all employees realize how their work serves the larger purpose and enables the company to be profitable, so it can keep creating jobs and investing in employees' growth and development.

At Aviall, our purpose was "Proudly keeping the world in flight." In those town hall meetings, we would share customer stories along with our metrics. We would speak about the airlines around the world that were relying on us, the military aircraft waiting to deploy, or the cargo operators that drive the global economy. Then I would explain why it matters that we provide same-day delivery of repair parts and why it's important that our shipping teams find, package, and ship an order within four hours of receiving it. Not only does it help us proudly keep the world in flight by improving our financial outcomes, it does so in a much more tangible way: the sooner those essential vehicles get their parts, the sooner they're back in the air.

Conduct Visual Meetings

When companies fail to communicate purpose or steer toward a clear direction, employees often perceive meetings as a waste of time. Complaints surface of meetings being repetitive, that nothing changes afterward, and that their contributions aren't considered or valued. In my experience, this type of feedback means one of two things: either the meetings truly are unnecessary, or the meetings are necessary, but their purpose as they relate to company objectives are unclear and they are ineffective at connecting employees and their contributions to those objectives. This outcome represents a wasted opportunity, as meetings, when executed properly, can make a tremendous positive impact. They unlock the potential of employees by guiding their strengths and efforts toward a shared goal.

Unnecessary meetings have a simple fix: have fewer meetings. Only get together when it's absolutely necessary, when decisions need to be made, problems need to be solved, and actions need to be taken. You can solve the second problem by documenting discussions on a whiteboard or virtual collaboration tool, such as Vibe. Whenever possible, I do this on a whiteboard, so I can document the discussion as it flows and incorporate as many perspectives as possible. For virtual teams, this can be done digitally. A visual aid helps break down complex problems. It promotes inclusion by bringing together different perspectives and conveys ideas in a way that grounds everyone in a common understanding. When you use a visual aid, employees have a chance to see how their contributions show up in the bigger conversation. A visual aid helps them see the progression of thoughts during a meeting, allowing them to draw a mental map of what was covered. The work that goes into drawing that map deepens understanding, which, in turn improves retention and helps prevent meetings where you keep mowing the same patch of grass.

If people are frustrated with the lack of action after meetings, then the problem stems from poor follow-through. Most of the time, this is a symptom of not having a clear understanding of the purpose of the meeting, the expected outcomes, or what needs to shift as a result. At the end of the meeting, document the discussion, decisions made, and next actions and steps. Then assign who will be responsible for each. That way, people within the team can support and hold each other accountable. Each member agrees to complete any assigned part and has the freedom to do it however that person chooses. Employees are encouraged to solicit the perspectives of any relevant stakeholders, even those in other departments, thereby incentivizing horizontal collaboration and discouraging a reliance on the corporate hierarchy.

At the next meeting, ask the point person on the project for an update and reflections, and find out whether that person needs any support. When this rhythm becomes established—task, attempt, report, support—it creates a predictability around your operations. If you stick to the rhythm consistently, delivering results in a repeatable way, it builds trust and allows you to lead change in a way that doesn't feel chaotic. If not, your consistency will falter, results will vary, and trust will erode.

Most of the whiteboard sessions that I have fall into one of three categories. In the first, we meet to discuss a specific issue that has been identified ahead of time. Everyone comes with a prepared position on how to address the issue. Then I start the meeting by drawing my thought process on the board. For example, I might draw our customers and identify the set I'm looking at, and then draw the supply chain and what value we are providing. After that, everyone else contributes thoughts and insights, which we use to edit mine. I'll erase, add, replace. Ideally, at the end, we have a plan that synthesizes all those different insights into one coordinated effort.

The second situation in which I incorporate a whiteboard is when an issue comes up during the course of a meeting that we need to solve on the spot. Usually this is driven by a missed goal or opportunity that someone brings up to improve our product or processes. As different perspectives pop up, I'll write the problem in the middle of the board, and then add each person's perspective around it. This has a number of benefits. For one, it assures everyone's voice is heard and valued. Second, it helps people process and integrate complex pieces of information. We retain only a small fraction of what we hear. When we forget information, it prevents us from building on or integrating it into our thought process. When employees can see everything that's been said in the meeting, they can improve their own contributions, and less time is consumed backtracking and answering clarifying questions.

Once the conversation runs its course, and we have everyone's initial insights on the board, I like to take a step back and read through what was said. Then I try to draw connections between the different lines of thought, find where our thinking intersects, and combine different perspectives until we end up with a couple of key themes that people agree on and that everyone understands completely.

In inclusive companies, where people share ideas freely, contradictory ideas might arise. The mere fact that disagreements exist might make employees uncomfortable, causing them to steer the conversation toward areas of consensus. This, while natural, often damages a company. The goal is to allow different perspectives, without letting them create barriers between teams or people that can't be crossed. To manage this, ask thoughtful questions to get as much information about the source of the disagreement on the board as possible. I always strip all of the emotion I can out of the statements as I write them on the board. While emotion can be a powerful motivator, it can also be disruptive. A neutral record of the disagreement helps people remember the substance, instead of the emotion attached to it. After diving deep into the diverging perspectives, you can draw connections between the competing viewpoints, and if necessary, invite people to continue the discussion outside the session.

Third, I sometimes lead meetings with a group of leaders, during which we discuss an adjustment to our strategy. Since all leaders must then implement what we discussed with their own teams, a visual aid generated at the meeting allows them to go back to their teams with a compelling story about why we're making that shift. This way, we can maintain alignment by making sure that each team receives the same set of key information.

It is even more valuable when employees can leave with a record of what we discussed. I'll often take a picture of the whiteboard when we finish a discussion, so that we all have an image that we can reference if needed. If we end up drawing a network diagram that shows how suppliers, customers, and our employees work together, or something similar, I'll take this a step further and ask someone to generate a graphic or handout of whatever we had on the board. These visual aids provide just enough of a trigger to help people remember exactly what was discussed, so that they can continue the conversation with their team and build on it.

Of course, leading these meetings makes it difficult to also participate in them. When you're focused on drawing out and synthesizing ideas, you can't always respond in the same way you would as a participant. For that reason, I, like many leaders, often will find someone else to facilitate. The best facilitators are good communicators, skilled listeners, people with prior experience facilitating meetings, who can distill complicated thoughts into a few manageable words on a whiteboard. I do my best to pick a facilitator who also works on the front lines, someone who has intimate contact with the problem we're trying to solve. The team leader usually meets with the facilitator prior to the meeting to map out a plan and set some goals. Going in with a plan and a clear understanding of the situation from the perspective of someone close to the opportunity is critical to a successful session.

Encourage Others to Lead and Leaders to Follow

Tapping a frontline leader to run a meeting, especially a meeting of "higher-ups" provides a host of added benefits. First, it helps engage the frontline workers in whatever solution the meeting develops. Second, it helps your front line gain experience leading at different levels. Third, it gives your upper managers experience following. You cannot be a good leader if you don't know how to follow. When executives find themselves in a meeting led by a frontline worker who is an expert in what he or she does, it helps those executives learn new perspectives, stay connected to the work, and hand over some of the decision-making power to the front lines. Fourth, it helps you find a better solution. Frontline workers offer a unique and holistic perspective of the day-to-day conditions of the business. They can use this to inform and guide the discussion, and even shape the bulk of what the solution will be.

In these situations, frontline leaders have an opportunity to develop their perspective, open with a complete view of the problem, and explain how they would fix it if they had unlimited resources at their disposal. Then our job as upper management is to provide a broader scope of data. We might say, "Well, here's how much money you do have," or "Here's some feedback from recent conversations with customers who say they prefer this specific thing. How does that alter our solution?"

Through this process, we can land on a solution that addresses all of the specific concerns and fits into the larger plans. At the same time, we're investing in our employees, training them to develop critical-thinking skills and make decisions on a company level.

This strategy also helps that frontline leader sell the new plan to the team. Instead of the plan being dictated from above, it's something that the team itself took the lead on and that has the full support of upper management. Similarly, it takes pressure off the middle managers, some of the most important and underappreciated members of most large companies. They usually feel pressure, both from frontline workers for pushing them too hard and from executive leadership for not producing better results. But when the frontline team plays a significant role in developing the plan and the goals, middle managers can shift their focus to leading horizontally and building bridges among teams.

That said, I need to make an important distinction: there's a big difference between a frontline team bringing a middle manager a problem to solve and a team bringing that same manager a solution that needs support. The first scenario usually is counterproductive: it takes away the opportunity for frontline managers to think through decisions on their own when they often have the best solutions. In the second scenario, middle managers can help frontline workers get what they need to be successful. While the frontline team is trying to implement the change, team members can come to the middle managers and say, "Hey, our software system isn't designed to handle the new product. What can we do to better understand our options?" or, "We're installing this new product, and we want to start rolling it out to some customers. Who else do we need to support while delivering this change to customers?" And then the middle manager, who should have relationships with managers in all of these departments, can go and make sure that each section of the company stays aligned through whatever change the frontline leaders implement. And the frontline employees, who so often feel forgotten, expendable, and unsupported, feel just the opposite.

It's simple, but saying, "We hear you, and we support you," and then following through, can completely transform someone's experience. That person will feel like a full member of a team, and, as a result, will want to invest in its success.

Create Project-Specific Waypoints
to Guide Progress

As you attempt to implement change, make sure that everyone understands where you're going, both in the short term and out into the future. This is especially important with large-scale over-hauls of operations, as huge projects can seem insurmountable and trigger anxiety. The more you can break a large-scale trans-formational project up into small, manageable parts, the more you can keep everyone motivated and moving in the right direc-tion. Further, because of the rate of change in the twenty-first century, it's essential to be able to modify the plan in response to unforeseen events. The old model, popularized in the 1980s and 1990s by the likes of then GE Chairman and CEO Jack Welch—of setting annual targets, breaking those down into quarterly goals, and then only checking in on the goals after long periods of time—is unsustainable. While long-term (e.g., five-year), annual, and quarterly goals are all still important, in the information age, you need to review and update them more frequently. In addition, it's vital that you allow for course corrections from the front lines that can respond to issues and developments as they occur, instead of waiting for a quarterly executive meeting. To ensure you make those course corrections, break any long-term goal down into weekly and even daily met-rics and have regular stand-up meetings to check progress. This will create the consistent, constructive habits that, when com-bined with clear goals, compound to spur radical growth.

Whenever I embark on a large project with my team, I always set a small, first-step goal that we can quickly achieve. Then we celebrate the success, debrief, and charge on to the next step. Early in my time at Honeywell, I saw this approach yield tremendous success. I worked in a division that made pres-sure switches for thermostats, and my boss at the time led our continuous improvement organization. Together, we set out to transform our division through the Six Sigma revolution, which focused on improving productivity, performance to customers, and employee engagement. The operation we oversaw was complex and crossed borders: each week, we produced 20,000 switch castings in a factory in San Diego. Then we shipped all of those across the border to one of five *maquiladoras* that we operated in Tijuana for assembly and testing, before shipping them back over the border and finally distributing them. In short, it was a situation with potential for misalignment at multiple stages. Not only did we have to coordinate six different factories, we had to do so in two different countries, in compliance with two sets of regulations, and with half our workforce speaking English and the other half speaking Spanish—all while producing nearly 100,000 units a month in a highly competitive market.

We had five KPIs where we wanted to see improvement: costs, quality, delivery, safety, and cycle time. We needed to get all 5,000 of the employees across all six sites to connect to these key metrics. So, for the next six months, we worked side by side with frontline teams at each site. We opened the first event by explaining that the objective of our Six Sigma revolution was for every employee to help create a better product, so we could be more competitive and lead change. Then we explained how this effort fit into the larger purpose of the company, which is "to create value for shareholders through control technology that saves energy, protects the environment, improves productivity, and increases comfort and safety."

The next step was to provide basic training on the Six Sigma problem-solving methodology, so everyone could engage with the process. Next, we began running weekly Kaizen events with each team. We taught them about the Kaizen continuous improvement practice, how you move from identifying a process failure to planning a solution, implementing that solution, checking the results, and course correcting where necessary.

After all that, we still didn't give the team leaders efficiency goals to hit. Instead, we engaged them in dialogue, and codeveloped smaller, specific frontline metrics for each team. Engaging the frontline employees in codeveloping goals is a vital step in the process. Not only does this train people to start thinking like leaders on their own, improving your company's ability to shift to a frontline leadership strategy, it also maximizes their engagement and accountability. People will try much harder to meet metrics that they themselves created.

At the end of those six months, with input from the frontline leaders as well as the financial, operational, and human resources teams, we developed a spreadsheet of five detailed metrics that those on the front lines could connect to. We made sure to develop the metrics/goals in a way that was consistent across all departments. For example, our goal was continuous improvement, not maintaining the status quo. We made sure that when the Human Resources team developed its performance review/ rating system and when the financial and operations teams developed their target metrics, they did so in a way that incentivized continuous improvement. This prevented competing or contradictory incentives, which would have pulled employees out of alignment and created a sense of confusion on the front lines.

After developing our goals, we posted them all on large boards at the entrance of each building to track progress. They were also posted on communication boards at the end of each assembly line, so that leaders could reference them during stand-up meetings.

This created alignment and a shared language among departments, which, in turn, allowed each team to develop its own innovations with little meddling from leadership. In a short time, the teams improved efficiency so much that we were able to shut down one of the factories.

This brings up an important point: undergoing this type of efficiency improvement or operational revamp can cause anxiety. All too often, companies undergo a transformation like this with the sole goal of driving up efficiency enough so they can cut staff and grow their profit margins. They forget the most important aspect of business: purpose. Your purpose should never be just to make more money. It should be to serve your customers and support your people the best that you can. If you can't connect an overhaul like the one we led in San Diego to the company's purpose, then the employees will suspect that it is an attempt to make their jobs obsolete. If they believe that, they'll never buy into an effort to improve efficiency. If anything, they will probably disengage from their jobs and become less efficient.

This is why we took pains to be in dialogue with our frontline employees and show them how our efforts connected to our purpose. And that only worked because the employees actually trusted us. Over time we had shown a consistent commitment to our purpose and concern for the well-being of our customers and our employees. This consistency built up a store of goodwill, so when we came to them to codevelop the plan, they trusted that they would benefit from their active participation. Because of our established practice of transferring talent to new sections of the company, they didn't worry that we would just let them go if we improved efficiency. It also helped that they knew that, even when we no longer needed somebody's services, we always provided as much support as possible.

As it turned out, this Honeywell restructuring did not result in any layoffs. We were able to transfer most of the workers from the closed sixth factory to one of the five we still operated, or to a different part of the company. Most of our cost savings came from the streamlined supply chain and the easier logistics and faster distribution this gave us. However, it doesn't always play out like this. Sometimes, a company has to become more efficient in a way that includes downsizing the workforce in order to survive. If you've established a solid bedrock of trust, you can still engage the employees as partners as you work toward improved performance. Most workers understand that in order for a company to offer what they want most—stability—the company must be profitable. If they trust the organization, and if the organization is transparent about the financial position and the need to make those changes, then most employees will understand—and they'll do whatever they can to help.

Take Advantage of the Changing Landscape

Once you've put in the groundwork necessary to maintain alignment, you'll be in a position to take advantage of the changing landscape. You'll be able to create an agile company, one that can respond to any given circumstance. In doing so, you'll make constant innovation within your company the new norm.

Innovation occurs on two different timescales. On one hand, there's the slow, methodical pace that comes from each team or employee making relatively small adjustments over time. On the other hand, there's the relatively fast, large-scale overhaul of an entire department, business, or industry that goes through many testing processes and iterations in a short period of time. In smaller, younger businesses, with condensed workforces and simple organizational structures, these two processes are more or less the same. Because these businesses don't have as many people to coordinate, they can try a new technique throughout the entire organization, see how it works for a week or a month, and then go back, tweak it, and instantly see the results of that tweak. If a new technology comes out that improves their processes, they can have a team explore how to incorporate it.

This is part of what makes small companies so much more agile than larger firms. Unless leaders take active steps to keep looking for better solutions, both types of innovation slow as the company grows. This is because processes become entrenched, so employees stop iterating their own individual jobs, and because any complete overhaul in the company requires a much greater investment of time and money, and therefore carries much more risk. They can't just test large-scale changes in the course of their normal operations, because if it doesn't work or if they have to make too many tweaks, it will throw the myriad of moving parts into chaos.

If a large company wants to be able to innovate and stay as agile as their smaller competitors, then they need to do two key things:

- Create a culture of innovation, in which each employee is encouraged and empowered to innovate.
- Intentionally invest in specific innovations in a way that doesn't interfere with operations.

Creating a Culture of Innovation

When business luminaries reminisce about their breakthrough ideas, they often ascribe their success to gut instinct. They'll say they just made the move that felt right, and then everything broke in their favor. Usually, this is only partially true, even if they believe it wholeheartedly. In reality, chalking these moves by chief executives up to instinct is a little like calling a Michael Jordan (the six-time NBA champion) game winner pure instinct.

There's a grain of truth (or else it wouldn't be a favorite cliché of sports announcers), as only MJ would know when to make his move, how to approach his man, create separation, and then take the shot. But much more important than the instinct was his *skill*. If that skill wasn't there, even with all of his innate killer instinct, he wouldn't have made so many shots. Even his instinct, that seemingly subconscious understanding of the game, could only exist because of his skill, which was so ingrained, it became second nature—and he could allow instinct to take over.

More often than not, this is the same thing that happens with innovation. As much as we like to think about innovation as a chance flash of brilliance, it is, in fact, a skill that can be cultivated. A company culture that encourages and teaches everyone how to innovate will create an army of frontline leaders who are adept at navigating the shifts.

The most earth-shattering innovations often come from an attempt to solve a problem or fill a unique customer need. The innovation comes in *response to* the outside world, not just from whomever comes up with the idea. For this reason, the best innovators usually are the people who excel at analyzing, understanding, and then responding to the world. They are the people who ask the deepest, boldest questions, who can develop both a broad and deep understanding of a specific issue and use that to fashion a response.

A culture that innovates with intention is one that encourages everyone to develop a broad and a deep understanding of any issue that comes up. The consequences for not doing this can be dire. Innovation requires investment, and if that investment doesn't yield new value, increased efficiency, or greater customer satisfaction, then it was wasted. Worse, companies that can't innovate and respond to the changing landscape will always see their market share dissolve until they disappear.

Get a 360-Degree View of the Problem

The business pioneer Steve Jobs described creativity as the ability to see connections between two things that no one else can see. In other words, creativity isn't developing a completely novel idea as much as it is taking two (or more) seemingly unrelated concepts, finding where they intersect, and letting the new idea come out of that intersection. These breakthroughs drove just about every phase of Apple's rise, in the big noticeable ways (e.g., the iPhone), as well as in the more minute details that separated Apple products from their early competitors. The only reason that the word processor on early Macs had multiple font options was because Jobs, while bumming around Reed College, stumbled into a calligraphy class. Years later, he remembered the beauty of calligraphy and the way the shape of the letters could alter the understanding of a text, and he insisted that the software developers add multiple font options. In order to have a chance to truly innovate, to draw novel connections between disparate ideas, you need to come into contact with different ideas and perspectives in the first place.

The whiteboard meetings I discuss don't just help maintain alignment, they also spur innovation by providing a 360-degree view of a problem and giving everyone an opportunity to contribute to a solution. If a company holds these sorts of meetings regularly, then it will create an environment that is constantly working toward solutions before issues snowball.

There are certain times when a process issue, market or environmental change, or shift from a competitor brings about a problem that urgently needs to be fixed. If the problem is minor, you can handle it with a whiteboard meeting, led by a frontline leader who understands the issue. To get a fully fleshed out understanding of a bigger issue, I like to use a process from Lean manufacturing practices called "the five whys." It's simple. I ask five "why" questions about the particular issue, with each question trying to get closer to the true root cause of the problem. Doing this helps to focus on solving the issue at its root cause instead of trying to treat the symptoms.

For a simple example, take something like an efficiency issue at a factory. The first question would be, "Why do we have this issue?"

If the answer is, "We don't have a good preventative maintenance plan to keep the machine calibrated," then the next question is, "Why don't we have a better maintenance plan?"

Then you get an answer like, "The maintenance manager who ran that left the company, and we haven't filled that role."

In this case, getting the machine calibrated once wouldn't fix the issue. A few months later, the machine would stop working again, and, in all likelihood, other pieces of equipment would start to fail as well. After uncovering the true issue, a vacancy in a key position, you can hire a new maintenance manager or transfer that responsibility to another person and have that person develop a proactive repair plan.

Often, frontline leaders will have the most success working on this kind of reconnaissance. They can leverage existing relationships with customers, distributors, suppliers, and fellow frontline workers to narrow in on the underlying issue, and they often can resolve the issues themselves, without input from middle managers or executives. This is another key benefit of the frontline leadership model—the ability to quickly innovate around problems—but like any of the others, it requires work to implement. This will only be effective if you've already connected each employee with the purpose of the company and shared enough information to keep everyone aligned. Then you need to allow employees to practice. When an issue comes up, ask an employee to investigate it, ask five whys, and solve it if possible. And if the employee can't, ask him or her to come back for support, and be ready to give as much as needed.

If a problem is larger, more complicated, or something you've tried to fix several times in the past but keep hitting the same roadblock, then you need a different approach that takes you into a deeper inquiry. While at Honeywell, I came up with a new approach that I call "the 50 questions."

At its most basic, it is exactly what it sounds like: I get as many people from different departments and backgrounds into a room as I possibly can, and I ask them every single question I can think of around the issue. Fifty is a good target number. Sometimes it can be more, rarely less. One of the primary goals of this approach is to get everyone to slow down and think through an issue from multiple angles.

Thought occurs on two levels: the faster, unconscious level as well as the slower, rational level. All sorts of unexamined biases control our fast thinking, and most of the quick decisions we make fall into old patterns of thought or fail to address the root of an issue, instead offering a cosmetic pseudo-solution. Because of the pace of business, most people rarely take the time necessary to slow down and think through a problem, which the 50 questions method forces you to do.

To guide my questioning, I use a framework, something like a SWOT (strengths, weaknesses, opportunities, threats) analysis, though I prefer a modified version of a balanced scorecard. Traditionally, that framework looks at an issue as it relates to four areas of running a company: financial, operational, employees, and customers. Depending on the situation, I've adapted the balanced scorecard approach to meet specific needs. For example, at Aviall, because it was particularly germane to my position, I added a fifth, environmental impact. With my work at SUMMi7, I've changed the fifth category to social impact.

I introduced the 50 questions methodology at Precision Conversions, a small company that converted old 757s into freight aircraft. We used this tool to address longstanding challenges, like aircraft manufacturing time. Every aircraft company perpetually looks for ways to reduce manufacturing times, mainly because the process takes so long. An aircraft can have up to four million individual parts, with a bill of material that runs seven or eight layers deep, meaning that you have parts that go into one assembly, and then into another level of assembly, and then another, and then another, and so on, until you reach seven subassemblies, all leading up to the final assembly. The longest part of this process is going from raw materials to completing all of the necessary subassemblies—that alone takes on average two or three years, depending on the aircraft. Because this process is so complicated, most people assume that they could never streamline it. Asking 50 questions about this process lifted us out of that fixed mindset. We'd first ask, "What would have to change for us to shave a year off the manufacturing time?"

Answer: "We'd have to have fewer layers in the bill of material, which would require us to manufacture differently."

Then we'd ask, "What can we change about manufacturing today?"

Answer: "3D printing or additive manufacturing, which would allow us to make complex assemblies in one piece, is becoming a more feasible and reliable option we could consider."

Then we can get more specific and ask what single component in the chain has the longest lead time. That would usually be the casting and forging, which also happen to be prime candidates for additive manufacturing.

In this case, although the technology might not be ready right away, we now have an option to pursue and invest in that will potentially reduce our lead times down the road. That leads us to a specific goal, something like getting all of the lead times in our process down to fewer than 100 days.

Next, we can look at every lead time more than 100 days and ask, "What would need to change to get us to our ambitious goal? How can we get there?"

We do that over and over and over again, and eventually a path emerges. It isn't necessarily a plan, but all of a sudden, we can see that something that seemed impossible is, in fact, achievable, and we can take the first couple of steps to get there.

Just taking those first steps sets off a process of continuous improvement, and maybe 2, 5, or even 10 years later, we reach a breakthrough and figure out how to make all of our castings with additive manufacturing. That's the kind of innovation that disrupts an entire industry. Everybody else might think it's a big revelation that came out of nowhere, but it was a long, concentrated grind that finally paid off.

This line of questioning only approaches the problem from an operational perspective. In a 50 questions session, we also would attack the issue from the other four perspectives on the scorecard (financial, employees, customers, and, on my scorecard, environmental impact). While the specific nature of the questions vary depending on the focus of each session, there are some core questions that stimulate the conversation and lead to deeper, more specific inquiries. These are:

- What would have to happen for this outcome to be true?
- What would make a customer choose a new product or service?
- How might our employees apply this process differently?
- If we didn't have any budget constraints, how would we approach this problem? If we didn't have time, resource, and space constraints? Any constraints?

- If we doubled our volume, what would be the first bottleneck?
- What is the biggest constraint that prevents us from producing more, faster? Do we need more machines? More people? People with different skill sets? Better tooling? Operating procedures?
- What different perspectives could come together to solve this differently?
- What is the sequence of our workflow? Is there a better way to organize that?
- What are the interdependencies between different processes and different ways that we develop our product? Can we streamline or remove those interdependencies?
- Where can we use information to better inform the activities that we're trying to do?
- What is it that we believe about our business that is holding us back?

You may ask some of these questions over and over again, each time going another level deeper. For example, you might ask, "What would have to be true for our desired outcomes to be possible?" Once you get an answer, you ask, "What needs to be true for *that* to be possible?" And so on.

While the example I give here looks at a long-term issue, this same process can yield positive results with short-term issues as well. A common example would be the transition to 5G capability that took off in 2020. The main advantage of 5G is that it allows for near real-time data transfer, with almost no lag.

This process also trains people to ask more and better questions. It helps them enter a perpetual growth mindset, one in which they constantly question their assumptions and beliefs about the world around them and look for ways to improve it.

This can extend beyond success in business, and can also help people slow down, empathize, and ask questions about the experience of others they meet from diverse backgrounds.

In business, they will learn what questions get the best result the fastest. Eventually, this will become so ingrained that when they encounter a complicated problem, the first thing that pops into their head won't be a floundering solution but 50 or 60 pointed questions. From there, they can gather information, map the landscape, and get to serious thinking and exploring while everyone else scrambles. In other words, they will master the art of asking questions to the point where they might change the face of an industry and ascribe it all to instinct.

No Stupid Questions, No Stupid Ideas

"What if we had a taxi company, without taxis?"

"What if we had a hotel company, without hotels?"

These questions, at first glance, sound like something a wide-eyed child would ask mother, only to get dismissed with something like, "That sounds neat!" As late as the 2000s, those ideas would have seemed completely impossible, yet each of these questions spawned companies whose worth exceeded tens of billions of dollars, Uber and Airbnb.

This is an important lesson: sometimes, the questions that seem the most naïve end up leading to the biggest innovations. It feels counterintuitive, but it makes sense. You'll never change the world if you don't question its most fundamental aspects.

To maximize innovation, create a culture on which no question or idea is bad. Not only will this allow employees to voice potentially world-alerting ideas, it will enable them to better develop their ideas. Very few ideas enter our minds fully formed. Most need a long process of reflection, attempted articulation, and refinement before they reach their full potential.

While people *can* do this alone, sharing ideas while they're still in development accelerates and enriches the thought process. I consider a meeting a success when my employees share ideas freely, think through things on the fly, and build off each other. This will never happen if they fear that any unpolished thought will be dismissed. Listen to and respect everyone's ideas, as they are shared, and ask thoughtful follow-up questions to help people refine their thinking.

Intentionally Invest in Innovation

No matter how well a company cultivates an innovative culture, it will still fall behind if it doesn't also look for opportunities to capitalize on big, rapid changes. Fortunately for larger companies, many of the same weaknesses that hold their innovative capabilities back—i.e., their size, success, and entrenchment—can be leveraged to fuel innovation. Smaller companies can iterate quickly, but they must do it at low cost. They don't always have the money or connections to procure the most recent technology, to hire the best talent, or to see an initiative through many iterations. A larger company has to use everything it has to invest in innovations in line with its purpose and values, which are most likely to help it serve its customers.

There are a few ways to do this. One common way for large companies is to create a venture capital arm that seeks out new companies to invest in, partner with, or buy. In this way, larger companies can benefit from the innovations of smaller ones, access new technology faster than their competitors, and use new technology to provide increased value to their customers or improve their internal processes.

Creating a venture capital arm requires deep pockets, and it wouldn't make sense for many medium or even some large businesses to invest in one. For example, at Aviall, we didn't have a venture capital arm. Instead, we divided our company into two parts, mode one and mode two. These two parts of our company operated largely independently of one another. Mode one handled our day-to-day business operations, where we did everything possible to create an innovating culture. Mode two was our research and development arm, which consisted of a small number of cross-functional experts who spent all of their time iterating and testing new technology, processes, and ideas. This group tested ideas as fast, or faster, than many small businesses, but without altering the function of the rest of the company until the group was sure that the new idea would be successful. The group learned, applied, learned, applied, learned, applied, sometimes through 100 iterations of the same idea, and then developed a rollout plan to bring it into the core business.

Finally, there is one key area where large companies can act as agents of change: through collaboration with their customers. I talk about this more in Chapter 6, but large companies can use the relationships they have with customers to solicit feedback that will guide their own change, and enter into partnerships that will help their customers grow. For example, at Aviall, we were working with multiple airlines and other partners to develop a road map that would leverage technology to better connect maintenance and supply chain activities across the industry. The goal was to support all stakeholders—our shareholders, employees, customers, and communities—by improving quality, safety, and sustainability. Customer collaboration results in a dynamic and symbiotic relationship, one that's built to last through periods of change. In fact, at their best, these relationships can spur mini-revolutions within the industry.

Your company can become the disruption that everyone else has to react to. At the end of the day, that's the best way to deal with change—by being the change.

6

CREATE A LEARNING ORGANIZATION

One of the beautiful characteristics of progress is that it accelerates. Increasingly, we are able to connect with and learn from more people who have access to a much greater cache of ideas than ever before. Those ideas can then inspire the next generation of thinkers. Albert Einstein didn't develop his theory of relativity in a vacuum. He drew on the work of earlier physicists, mathematicians like Marcel Grossmann and Tullio Levi-Civita, and even the science fiction author Felix Eberty, who wrote about traveling faster than light, and used it to move our understanding of the world forward.

The same process plays out in every business every single day. In fact, this process is the most important part of any business. As Jack Welch said, "An organization's ability to learn, and translate that learning into action rapidly, is the ultimate competitive advantage."* In my experience, that's proven true. Organizations that create a culture of learning improve profit

---

* Robert Slater, *Jack Welch and the GE Way: Management Insights and Leadership Secrets of the Legendary CEO* (New York: McGraw-Hill Education, 1998), 12.

margins by discovering ways to reduce costs and adapt to changing customer needs. The opportunity to learn motivates employees to give their full effort at work. And when everyone engages in perpetual self-improvement, the company rarely outgrows its leadership. Instead, employees grow with the company. The company develops internal talent instead of going through a costly leadership change each time it enters new territory. And finally, when a company pools together all of its knowledge, it will create better solutions that take into account the full complexities of the situation, power innovation and growth, and improve customer satisfaction.

Creating a learning organization takes two main actions:

- Encourage each individual employee to learn.
- Facilitate companywide learning by putting systems in place.

Encourage Employee Learning

An organization is nothing without its people. Therefore, the first step in creating a learning organization is to make sure that each employee is engaged in a constant process of discovery and growth. Not only will this improve the technical capability of your workforce, it will also prime employees to look constantly for opportunities to refine and improve, which will help cultivate a learning organization. I've found three keys to encouraging each employee to learn:

- Create a workplace environment in which employees feel supported enough to learn.
- Promote personal development plans.
- Facilitate frontline learning.

Support Your Employees

It requires more effort and vulnerability to learn and grow than to remain stagnant. Employees won't take on this extra work and risk if they don't feel supported in their efforts, so before anything else, you must create a supportive workplace. Fortunately, much of what I've discussed in this book will help you build that kind of ecosystem.

One of the greatest questions an employee can ask to drive growth is, "How can I do my job a little better?" Employees who think like this do more creative and proactive work. They don't just come to work, tick off all the boxes on their to-do lists, and leave. Employees will only ask that question if they feel motivated enough to go the extra mile. As I've covered, purpose is one of the best motivators. When you take steps to connect employees with purpose, like those described in Chapter 2, you will encourage learning. Purpose keeps employees engaged enough to put in the extra effort, and gives them a goal to strive for.

Next, learning requires time: time to think, time to try new things, and even time to fail. A company in which employees are constantly running around putting out fires or spending every moment of their time accomplishing their daily tasks will never foster learning. A learning organization will free up time for reflection and growth by having a well-established and efficient operating rhythm. Schedule time to bring teams together to brainstorm solutions to a problem. Make it a daily habit to come in every morning and discuss how the previous day went and what you can learn and apply from it. Get away from work for a day at the start of the year to review what worked well and didn't work well the previous year, as well as what changes you'll commit to in order to learn and perform even better.

Finally, a learning organization leverages the expertise of its most experienced employees. At Aviall, we accomplished this with an annual celebration for 30-year employees. During this dinner event, we thanked them for their service and asked for their help. As the CEO, I'd give a speech in which I reminded them that they are the stewards of our company's culture, and it's been through their hard-earned skill and openness to change that our company has grown. Then I'd ask them to share their knowledge with our new employees. And because we'd proven time and again our investment in them, our senior employees invested in our continued success. This mutual investment grew out of genuine concern for each other's future, and is a critical component of a learning organization.

Promote Personal Development Plans

Any itinerary or plan requires a clear starting point. You'll never know the next step toward your goal if you don't know where you are. The same is true for personal development plans—you can never know what new training or experiences to seek out until you know your strengths and weaknesses. Yet, as Whitney Johnson, author and one of the 50 leading business thinkers in the world according to Thinkers50, points out, most of us don't know our own strengths. One of the most important things any leader can do is help employees identify their superpowers. This has two benefits. First, employees will better leverage their strengths in their work. Second, it will help them develop a coherent personal development plan, one that builds on their natural skills and aligns with their personal ambitions, as well as those of the company.

Of course, leaders can and should help them create those plans. I started hosting career coaching sessions in 2000, during my time at Honeywell. I would meet with a group of employees every week and help them plan their careers. These sessions arose organically. I'd been talking to my employees (it's impossible to overstate the value of just talking to your employees) about how I didn't agree with the baby boomer idea of a "natural career ladder," in which jobs depend almost entirely on the people you know, and you climb from connection to connection. I told them about my methodical approach to my career, how I map out five-year mini careers, identifying where I want to be at the end of five years and the skills needed to reach my goal. Word spread about these meetings, and more and more employees showed up, and a network of peer support emerged for new employees that wanted to feel more empowered over their own career path.

When I help an employee develop a plan, I like to remind people to consider that the rate of change in the twenty-first century has caused companies to retool far more often than ever before. This constant shifting, while necessary for company survival, makes it more difficult for people who don't have the skills to adapt to remain competitive. I advise and support all of my employees to invest some time and/or money learning finance or operations management, even if their primary interest is marketing. If they don't, they risk becoming specialists, with a narrow job description that might get iterated out of usefulness in the next few years. Of course, I always prioritize their goals and purpose when developing plans, but with an expanded lens to consider around learning agility.

These development sessions become even more useful when paired with real institutional support. Businesses should strive to build into their business plans the ability to provide employees the money and time needed to develop the skills that will best serve them in the long run. Not only will this investment show your employees that you care, further increasing their engagement, the company also will reap the benefits from those new skills. This is far more effective than continuously bringing in new employees as skill needs change.

Facilitate Learning on the Front Lines

Our goal as leaders should be to empower people, and nothing disperses power better than education. I mean that in a traditional sense (i.e., public school, college) but also in the workforce. Before frontline workers can become decision-making frontline leaders, they need a certain amount of knowledge. They need education. What I'm describing goes deeper than acquiring new hard or soft skills. While those skills always help, employees need to know broad context about the company as it relates to their jobs. They should be able to answer all of these questions: What market are we in? What is our purpose within the market? Who are our customers, and what do they do? What problem do we solve for them? What is our business model? How do all of the activities in the company fit together?

Once frontline employees understand all of this, they will find opportunities for improvement and feel more confident in their abilities to make decisions that won't yank the company off course. From there, they can practice frontline leadership. This creates a positive feedback loop: the more practice they have making decisions, the more they will learn. Because education disperses power, the more they learn, the more they will grow into frontline leaders.

To speed up this feedback loop, leaders should do two things: give their employees access to the same context or information that "upper" management uses to make decisions, and teach their employees critical-thinking skills that will allow them to process the information.

The first step of this process—sharing context—harkens back to radical transparency. Whenever leaders discuss a decision with their teams, they should divulge every pertinent piece of information. What is the state of the business? What's on their mind as a leader? What are the opportunities and risks in front of the company? This is a sort of "we-are-here" conversation that situates the company in relation to its goals. Even sharing this much information will develop the critical-thinking and decision-making skills of frontline employees because the leader demonstrates how to sift through the wealth of information to find the key bits to consider.

In these meetings, leaders also ought to make sure that everyone understands how he or she connects to the overall goals. In other words, make sure employees understand their positions within the company, why they are a vital part of the flow of business, and what is needed from them to move forward. That way, when they return to work, they understand their individual goals and the whole project, and they can iterate their own process.

Sharing this information will give frontline employees the tools they need to operate as frontline leaders and begin to train them to think critically. But to really develop their decision-making, they actually need to make decisions. For most senior managers and owners, this spurs anxiety. What if the employees make the wrong decisions? What if it ruins the company? Leads to rampant misalignment?

My response to this goes back to my definition of leadership: a leader's goal should be to empower others. If that's what you believe and how you act, then the downsides from an occasional misstep by an employee will be vastly outweighed by the benefits of an empowered, engaged, learning, and innovating workforce. On the other hand, if you believe that leadership means making all of the decisions, then you do a disservice to the company and to yourself. Eventually, the stress of always having the final say will lead to decision fatigue and burnout. It will lead to poor decisions.

Worse, this sort of need for control will arrest the development of the whole company. Innovation is collaborative and usually happens on the front lines. One leader in a company can't be responsible for all of the innovation. Not even Steve Jobs, one of the most storied innovators in American history, put that much pressure on himself. Most early Apple employees describe his genius as his ability to inspire his employees to think bigger, not to have all of the best ideas himself. The concentration of power in the hands of a few hampers day-to-day operations. When everything goes through one or two overtasked leaders, those people become bottlenecks, and nothing gets done.

Of course, the flaws of this management style manifest before work bottlenecks around the swamped leader. The central assumption—that it's the bigwigs who make the best choices—is incorrect. The person best equipped to solve a problem is the person closest to that problem. That employee knows the most about the intricacies of the issue and the process involved in the problem and has the relationships with other workers and customers needed to best solve the problem. The goal should always be to empower employees with as much information as possible, let them make the decisions, and then encourage them to ask for help if they need it.

In my experience, frontline workers make fewer mistakes than middle managers do in these situations. But they will make mistakes. Luckily, because most frontline employees make decisions about what's directly in front of them, it's rare for those mistakes to cause irreperable damage. Beyond that, each of those mistakes will accelerate the learning process for that employee.

Guide with Questions

You, as a leader, can also work to limit the severity of the mistakes and maximize learning. First, make sure that you have a successful, established operating rhythm, with regular meetings to check in on goals and offer support throughout the process. Ideally and particularly for employees who don't have a lot of experience making decisions, use those meetings to make sure they are grounded in the purpose and the goals of the company, before they take any action. When someone brings a specific idea up in a meeting, ask questions like: "What are you trying to solve? Are you trying to improve customer engagement? What is the problem with customer engagement? Do you have data that shows where we are today in customer engagement, and a specific, measurable improvement you want to see? Do you have real customer insights that you can integrate into your solution?"

The above is just an example of the type of questions I might ask—the questions will change depending on the situation. I use these questions to accomplish two things: first, to make sure employees have applied enough thought to the proposed idea before executing it, and second, to model how I would approach making this decision. I try to strike a balance between teaching and empowering. I offer guidance without disparaging their ideas or swooping in with my own proposal, which likely wouldn't be as good as theirs.

Continue providing that support after the initial meeting. This is where the established operating rhythm of the company— whether through daily or weekly check-ins—comes in. Once they've established goals, put those goals up on the board, break them down into smaller pieces and incremental commitments, and ask how each of those are going. Ask where there are gaps, and where the frontline employees might need some assistance.

While they're answering the questions, frontline employees might say that they didn't meet a goal, but not offer a full explanation why or a plan for how they will correct this. Often, this happens with employees who are not used to operating as a frontline leader. In that case, I usually follow up with a line of questioning like, "Well, why didn't you hit that goal?" They may say something like, "Somebody called in sick." I would then ask, "Do we know why they called in sick? When did we know they couldn't come to work? Was there an opportunity to bring someone in from a different department to cover the missing employee's work?" If they reply along the lines of, "We probably could have found someone to cover. We just didn't think of it," then they've learned two things. First, they've learned to always have a backup plan. Second, they've learned to look for a way to work around problems that come up. This sets your expectation for them to take more initiative and to think like problem solvers in their own right.

If their response is, "No, that wouldn't have worked because the person who called in sick does a very specific job that nobody else knows," then it's a different conversation. I would then ask something like, "What program can we put into place to make sure that we always have someone who can step in?" These lines of questioning teach the team members to identify the root cause of the delay and develop a solution. After a few of these meetings, they will do this without your guidance.

The beauty of this is that as people learn, they become more engaged, more proactive, and more motivated at work. Multiple studies have shown that the three biggest factors that determine motivation are mastery, purpose, and autonomy. For me, personally, this is true. Every time I start something, I want to master it. It's why I love running so much. I can measure my rate and my distance, and push myself to go a little faster and a little farther with each run. In terms of autonomy, I, like most people, feel much more rewarded when I accomplish my task my own way. It allows me to bring my full mastery to bear on a situation, and develop a method of working that best suits me. And purpose is the ultimate motivator. This management style combines all three. It encourages all employees to constantly get better, to do so on their terms, in pursuit of their and the company's purpose. The end result is an incredibly motivated team.

Facilitate Companywide Learning

Once everyone in the organization is empowered to learn, the next step to develop a learning culture is to create an environment of collective learning and knowledge sharing. From what I've observed, most organizations only leverage about 30 percent of their collective knowledge. There are a number of reasons for this, but they all boil down to the fact that organizations don't know what they know. The information stays bottled up in specific departments or even specific employees' heads, instead of flowing throughout the organization and guiding decisions. To combat this, find ways to tap into the full extent of an employee's knowledge and expertise, and help that employee to teach and coach fellow coworkers. This is collective learning, and there are six main ways to accomplish it:

- Speak the same language.
- Combine perspectives.
- Promote generalists.
- Create knowledge networks.
- Use frontline expertise.
- Develop grit.

Speak the Same Language

For collective learning to work, each employee needs to be both a teacher and a student—that includes the most senior leaders. Ideally, the organization functions as a giant pool of knowledge that any employee can tap into at any time, and peers help guide each other in the acquisition of new proficiencies—all while working together to develop innovative solutions to the problems that come up. During my time at Honeywell, I learned that none of this was possible without developing a shared business language that employees could use to exchange information and collaborate among departments. A shared language has other huge benefits: it unifies the company and allows employees to stay motivated and grow during periods of adversity, instead of buckling.

I say this because a year into my time at Honeywell, New York City's Twin Towers were tragically brought down. It was a time of great collective grieving for our nation. It was also a time of distress for members of the aviation industry, including Honeywell. But because of our unity, shared purpose, common language, and commitment to continual learning, we were able to navigate the fallout of that tragedy and come out stronger than ever. In the period after 9/11, we launched many successful new products, including the HTF700 engine, which is used on the Bombardier, Gulfstream, and Embraer jets. That said, this accomplishment pales in comparison to the legacy of all the leaders who cut their teeth in this department at this time, many of whom went on to hold influential positions in the industry.

We owed a large portion of our success to our strong foundation of learning, which we built around a shared language. We borrowed that language from an organization, APICS (now the Association for Supply Chain Management), that sets global standards for supply chain learning, language, and process architecture. From this organization, we also took an operational framework, or a set of standards and goals, that our employees could use to analyze what was happening within the company. In the information age, such a framework is vital. It allows people to zero in on the signal in the noise.

We combined these standards, norms, and vocabulary with the Six Sigma problem-solving methodology—which I described earlier and is widely used across industries. Each of the thousands of employees in the entire integrated supply chain, which included manufacturing, procurement, logistics, and all related functions, had to master these two systems. Once employees achieved a certain degree of skill with the respective systems, they taught their peers. Not only did this reinforce their understanding of the content, it also helped strengthen relationships within the workforce. The end result was a resilient, connected, collaborative team that could communicate effectively, innovate with precision, and share information across departments.

When I got to L3 in 2008, I knew I wanted to replicate the learning environment from Honeywell. I'd never previously held a position that carried more responsibility than my job at L3: we supported aircraft around the world, many belonging to militaries, police forces, and even heads of state. These aircraft operated in volatile environments, and we needed to be agile enough to respond to our customers' needs as they arose. I had a strong team, composed of many veterans with a deep knowledge base in logistics. But up to that point, it hadn't been fully leveraged. With the support of the leadership team, we decided to pool all that knowledge together in a collaborative problem-solving model.

After the success at Honeywell, I chose the Six Sigma training model as the base and combined it with Lean manufacturing methodology. Again, we trained every employee in our model, and launched projects that would lead change. One of the very first projects mapped the flow of landing gear throughout our 20,000-square-foot facility as we repaired the gear. We wanted to see if we were wasting any time by moving the parts around more than was necessary. When the team members reported back, they revealed that a unit we repaired traveled more than 5,000 feet to be assembled. That distance was greater than the runway at the local airport, and was the rough equivalent of circling our building *15 times!* This made everyone realize the effectiveness of our methodology, and our war on waste began. Over the next year, we trained dozens of people, launched many more projects, and saw double-digit improvements through lower inventory, increased volume, lower cost, and better delivery performance—all led by our frontline teams.

Combine Perspectives

Often, the best solution to a problem is one that combines aspects from three or four unique perspectives. However, people tend to focus on areas of agreement in meetings, which quashes debate and keeps diverse perspectives locked up. This is part of how that 70 percent of knowledge never gets used—people either don't want to or don't think to share it, especially if it might cause conflict. And if knowledge doesn't flow, it can't spark creativity. People do their best creative thinking when they go into a conversation with an open mind and are forced to respond to foreign ideas. It's how many of the best innovations in history have come about—when someone applied an old idea in a new context, to a new problem, or in a new industry. Your ability to be creative grows with the knowledge base that you draw from, and when people don't share their unique perspectives, they ultimately limit the knowledge base.

Leaders must do everything they can to draw out these perspectives. Two of my favorite ways to do this happens before meetings. First, I tell all of my employees what we will discuss at the meeting and ask them to show up with a well-thought-out position on the subject. This elevates the level of discussion and allows everyone to offer real, unique thoughts instead of knee-jerk reactions. Second, I review the list of employees who will attend, and then come up with one or two targeted questions for each of them that references something in their past. For example, I might ask one employee, "If you were still at GE, how would you have solved this?" or, "Based on your time working in finance, what do you think our best solution is?"

In the same way I work to draw from everyone's past experience, and from as many fields of study as possible. I make it a point to know a tiny bit about what each of my employees chose to study, what their specific interests and passions are, whether they be marketing, finance, operations, or even fields that are less explicitly related to business, like psychology or human behavior. This has many benefits: one of the biggest is that it helps develop a solution that is not only richer but facilitates empathy and a deeper understanding of people. A *human* solution, not a merely technical one. Companies often get so caught up in the theories about design, marketing, and business that they forget that the ultimate goal is to create more value for customers, not to achieve some abstract ideal of efficiency.

Dipping into knowledge pools beyond the confines of business helps with this. I work to train myself to think like this by always reading three or four books about different fields at a time. For example, I may be reading a business book, a history book, and a philosophy book. As I read, I try to connect the dots between the different fields. Maybe an anecdote about Abraham Lincoln illustrates a point about leadership from the business book. Maybe a metaphysical stance in the philosophy book helps me refine or expand my values, my thinking about radical transparency, or my approach to business. Almost everyone is an expert in at least one or two areas that seem completely unrelated to their jobs. A learning organization draws on all those passions to better inform their solutions.

That said, it's impossible to know every part of someone's personal history. I know that these pointed questions won't necessarily lead to an immediate solution. But just by asking them, people are encouraged to think in more expansive ways. Suddenly, they don't just consider the issue from Aviall's perspective, but from their own, and they draw on their own history and experience. That minor suggestion can stir up the subconscious and make it search through memories for something that might apply in the present moment. After asking a few of these more personal questions to bring out unique perspectives and getting the juices flowing through everyone's minds, I like to switch and ask broader, open-ended questions that reframe the issue. Let's say that a customer is unhappy with the delivery of its products. I'll ask questions like, "Have you spoken to the customer? What did the customer say? Based on what was said, what can we do differently? If we make that change and establish a new expectation with the customer, will it actually solve the problem or just a be a temporary fix?"

The questions vary depending on the situation, but the overriding goal is to develop a deeper understanding of the problem, centered on the customer's experience, while being open-ended enough for everyone to contribute personal perspectives. Once employees respond, I pull out the whiteboard and hunt for points of intersection to create the best possible solution.

Find and Promote Generalists

The best solution in the world still needs to be communicated to be effective. This is one of the reasons that generalists—employees with a background in a wide variety of fields—are particularly important. Not only can they draw on their diverse experiences to help develop holistic solutions to complicated, multifaceted problems, they are also able to communicate those solutions to various departments in a comprehensible way that ensures alignment.

In the twenty-first century, the problems that we face as individuals and as businesses are more complicated and inter-connected than ever before. Most colleges, universities, and business schools can only do so much to prepare students for the diverse range of issues they'll face. Then they enter the workforce and end up in a career track of similar jobs because we tend to migrate toward what's familiar to us and what we feel quali-fied for. It's how the traditional career ladder worked during the past century when companies provided a level of stability that's difficult to find today. The end result is that most companies struggle with a dearth of generalists at a time when they are more vital to an organization than ever before.

Companies can and should develop their own generalists to help connect teams and departments together. A great way to do this is through a rotation or shadowing program. Early in my career, at Honeywell, I participated in one of these rotation programs, called Pathways. It exposed me to a range of differ-ent jobs and different countries, namely, Mexico and China. In both locations, with the help of an interpreter, I had the chance to teach our teams a variety of subjects, including how to imple-ment a Lean manufacturing approach. I credit much of my success to this experience. Not only did I gain new technical expertise, I also became comfortable adapting to change and working with a diverse group of people. I gained a humbling degree of cultural awareness and discovered some of my most important personal values. Finally, the opportunity to make a positive impact in parts of the world that traditionally don't have access to the same opportunities we have in the United States motivated me and made my work feel truly rewarding. These types of programs, as well as helping employees consciously develop broad skill sets, will allow you to nurture the generalists that can facilitate the flow of information among departments and encourage collective learning.

Create Knowledge Networks

Adhering to a strict, hierarchical chain of command prevents companies from leveraging all of their knowledge. I've already discussed how empowering frontline employees unlocks their unique expertise, but even that isn't enough to solve the problem. Eventually, a customer will have an issue or a request that falls beyond the scope of a frontline employee's expertise. Take, for example, something like blockchain, a very specific, highly complicated, game-changing bit of technology. Few frontline employees are likely equiped to discuss blockchain with a customer who wants to integrate it into its operations. Most frontline employees would pass this request up the chain of command to their manager. The problem is, those middle managers probably know as much, if not less, about blockchain than the frontline workers. The manager might tell the customer something like, "I'm not sure that we can help," or might promise to look into it, but never get around to it. The customer either never gets a solution or has to wait for it. The longer a customer waits, the more opportunity a competitor has to offer that customer what it needs, snagging the business.

During this entire show of ineffectiveness, there's probably at least one or two people in the organization—maybe in the IT department, maybe in accounting—who are experts in blockchain. But since it isn't part of their job description, nobody else in the company knows, and nobody thinks to ask. The customer's request goes unsatisfied, and we lose that opportunity. If this becomes a pattern for the company, eventually that customer and many others will leave.

Creating a Knowledge Network is a simple way to combat this. Essentially, a Knowledge Network is an informal internal group for employees with shared interests to gather and learn from one another. It's a community of practice, supported and facilitated by the company. For example, at Aviall, we noticed that a lot of our employees were interested in blockchain, so we created an internal collaboration website, only available to Aviall employees, where they could log on and share ideas about the technology. We've similarly created the infrastructure for other groups with different interests.

Now, let's say the same hypothetical happens at Aviall, and a customer asks about integrating blockchain technology into its systems. The frontline employee doesn't even have to bring it up with a manager—he or she can go straight to this internal community of practice and say, "Hey, our customer thinks that blockchain might really help it. Is it feasible? Is there any way we can do that?" Suddenly, experts in the company, no matter what department they work in or what country they live in, can offer their own potential solution. Within weeks or even days, the frontline employee might be able to go to the customer and say, "We're working on it. It seems like we might be able to do this for you. Would that fit your needs?" The employees of the company learn from each other and innovate new solutions with impressive agility and without getting leadership involved at all. That sort of rapid response will retain customers, and is only possible in a learning organization that practices frontline leadership.

Use Frontline Expertise

Thomas Edison said, "Genius is 1 percent inspiration, 99 percent perspiration." In a company, all of that perspiration happens on the front lines. By that, I mean that change and innovation occurs differently at different levels of the company. Leaders and more established executives learn and innovate mostly by talking to other leaders, looking at numbers, and trying to figure out how best to position the company. That serves as the inspiration. But if the leadership team ever wants to actually implement one of their ideas, to change the course of the company, they'll need to get the frontline team to do something different. And often, it's the frontline team that drives the change. These are the teams that identify how to make change happen and find new ways to work. That's the perspiration.

This is an important consideration in relation to automation. As soon as you automate something, you remove the human element and therefore the potential for innovation. This can be acceptable for extremely repetitive, unchanging core tasks. But if you want to keep growing in an area, you need workers who "sweat the details" every day to get better.

The perspiration is the real hard work of any change in business: building something differently, designing a different product, delivering a different solution. The front line is the starting point of the company. It's the font line's effort that will actually change the company's trajectory. For example, in aviation, there's at least one chemical used in every maintenance task on an aircraft. Those chemicals are hard to handle, making any supply chain for the chemicals complicated. At Aviall, we realized that we could teach each customer how to properly store the chemicals. Doing this would help our customers manage those chemicals in a more environmentally friendly way, improve worker safety, and reduce waste.

To build that solution, we went to the supply chain. At our warehouse, where we store and ship more than 100,000 different chemicals, every chemical has a different MSDS information card with handling instructions. For almost anyone else, this is an overwhelming amount of data. But for our warehouse workers, it's second nature. They're experts. They can look at a bottle and say, "Oh, paint. This is how you pack paint, this is the labeling, these are the temperature requirements for storage and shipping. Oh, oil. You can't ship that by air. Here's how you pack that."

We used the knowledge already in our frontline employees' heads to map out how all of these chemicals flowed, what regulations governed their use, and how best to handle and dispose of them. We then built that into a software system and shared it with our customers, so that whenever they received a chemical from us, they knew how to handle it. By sharing our knowledge with them, we extended our learning culture to our customers. None of that would have been possible if we hadn't learned and leveraged the knowledge held by our front lines.

Develop Grit

I mentioned earlier that our learning culture helped us weather the post-9/11 storm at Honeywell. That's true, but I want to take it even further. A true learning organization doesn't just survive adversity, it absorbs the adversity and uses it to propel new learning and new growth. That's how you truly overcome. At the root of that is grit, which Angela Duckworth, author of *Grit,* defines as "passion and perseverance for very long-term goals. Grit is having stamina. Grit is sticking with your future, day in, day out, not just for the week, not just for the month, but for years, and working really hard to make that future a reality. Grit is living life like it's a marathon, not a sprint." Or, in simpler terms, selfless and stubborn resilience. It means inspiring your team with clear long-term goals, a meaningful purpose, collective learning and growth, and the belief that people can make a difference with their contributions. If you can do that, you can unlock the full potential of your organization and achieve more than any past precedence would suggest.

As I wrote this book, I went through one of the most challenging periods of my career—when I left the corporate world to start SUMMi7. For the first time in 25 years, I didn't have a stable paycheck or a predictable income, and I still had three kids to support. It felt like a tremendous risk, and in the early days I struggled with a bit of impostor syndrome. New businesses face several hurdles before they reach stability and profitability, and there were moments when I feared we would fail. In those times, I had to set organizational guidelines and goals, and then just bear down, work hard, and rely on grit and perseverance—all while trusting that I had the wisdom to pivot when necessary.

7

REMOVE COMPLEXITY

As companies grow, they become more complex. For example, at the founding of my company, SUMMi7, we had five team members, including myself. All five of us interacted with each of our customers; so, we knew what they needed and wanted. Because of this, in meetings we could always center our efforts on our customers and their needs. I had the opportunity to speak to clients directly, and I could adjust our strategies to take into account what they said.

As we grew, we needed more than five people to handle our operations. Our chief operating officer couldn't also serve as chief marketing officer; we added managers, some frontline employees, and a sales team. Eventually, the plan is to have multiple departments, with teams of 10 or more people in each. When we get to that point, I, as the CEO, will no longer have a direct line of sight to the customer. In fact, I may be a dozen or so steps removed from the customer. And all of the other managers, the other members of the founding team, and the senior executives also will have less direct contact with customers. As a result, it will be harder for us to see them. At this level of growth, when the executive team gets together to meet and strategize, we won't all have spoken to all of our customers, and we will be making decisions with less direct knowledge of the customer.

Greater distance from customers is just one of the many types of complexities that companies accumulate as they grow. Some operational complexity is necessary to handle growth, but too much can cause all sorts of problems—from increased costs to reduced competitiveness in the marketplace. The sum of this can ruin a business.

One layer of complexity that seeps into companies once they've become established is outdated technology. Technology advances so quickly that whatever software and hardware we use today will be outdated within the next decade, possibly sooner. This can be one of the greatest drivers of complexity— as technology ages, it becomes harder for a younger, more savvy generation to plug into old processes. Companies that don't invest in new technology tend to spend greater amounts of time training their new employees to use outdated processes. The equipment will break down, the software won't integrate, your company ends up wasting countless hours on repairs, and over-head costs rise.

Another layer of complexity emerges over the course of decades, during which hundreds of employees will have come and gone. Each one of them will have had a unique way of doing things, often developed in response to the unique challenges that faced the company during that employee's tenure. I'm a firm believer that the best way to do a job is the way that feels best to the person doing it, so it's good that these employees generate their own best practices. But some of these personally customized processes will stick around long after the employee leaves. They will become dogma, something that each new hire has to learn and something that, more often than not, will feel archaic, arbitrary, and inefficient.

This is a natural part of the aging process of a company, and like aging in humans, it can't be avoided. But just as a proper diet and solid exercise can slow or even reverse the development of plaque in your arteries, the right steps taken by a company can prevent "organizational plaque," the needless complexities that block the flow of information and innovation. A streamlined company can better hear and respond to the voice of the customer, and it can innovate purposefully, in a way that grows profits without sacrificing core values and commitments. There are three main keys to removing complexity:

- Let the customer be your guide.
- Look for areas to simplify.
- Manage the changes that remove complexity.

Let the Customer Be Your Guide

Be aware that the customer's wants and needs are the most important considerations in any business operational change, and simplification is no different. Doing so will cut through complexity, and give you a strong grasp on where you stand and where you need to go. It will also show you exactly what makes your company unique—and reveal the few inviolable aspects of your brand that you must protect in any efficiency crusade.

Your ability to hear your customer's voice is key to your success. When I say "voice," I don't mean something general, like "feedback" or "input." I mean this literally: you should do everything you can to actually *hear* what customers say, in their own words. When you can't speak to them face-to-face, the next best thing is a word-for-word transcription, not a summary. Aggregated or summarized customer feedback can actually *add* complexity. For example, let's say a customer says, "I really loved the efficiency of the delivery and the intuitive design of the product."

If the customer relations team just summarizes that as, "Great job," then nobody on the product development or delivery teams knows what went well. They can't see what to improve and what to leave as is. Thus, partial information gums up the innovating capacity of the entire team.

In addition to greater clarity, when you capture information in a customer's voice, it will help you develop an emotional connection with that customer. This is critical. Humans are emotional creatures. We make so few of our decisions based on "rational" thinking. In fact, most of our purchasing decisions are emotionally motivated. Maybe it's a memory of always eating a certain kind of cake at your birthday parties, or a certain brand of soda pop that reminds you of your grandparents. These emotional resonances subtly drive our decision-making, especially in markets where other considerations—price, convenience, quality—are more or less uniform.

I personally make a lot of consumer choices this way. For example, my favorite dessert is ice cream. I've loved it my entire life, and both of my kids, as most kids do, also love ice cream. For years, we always bought the same brand of ice cream because it came in these little, single-serve, premade sundaes. The sundaes had different flavors, so you might get vanilla with fudge sauce and peanuts, or chocolate with marshmallow sauce, or strawberry with fudge. Each night after dinner, my kids and I ate our own single-serve sundaes. They were perfect because one was enough for each of us, and we could talk about our favorite flavors, taste each other's, and compare. It didn't require a lot of preparation or clean up. The ice cream wasn't fabulous, but it was good, and more importantly, it was a beautiful moment to share with my kids. That's why I bought the ice cream—not because of price or even the convenience, but for the ritual. Then the ice cream company stopped selling single-serve sundaes! Their replacement product was a little cheaper because the company saved money on packaging, but I stopped buying it because it no longer filled the same emotional need.

As a baseline, an organization should expect all employees to establish a robust, lasting connection with their customers. Then put in place the infrastructure to make it possible. There are a couple of ways to do this. In meetings with senior leadership, make it a habit to go directly to the source to find ways to improve your products and services. This involves bringing in customers and having them talk to our executives about their lives. The executives come loaded with questions—about a customer's operations, the biggest challenges it faces, the one thing they might change about the product or its customer experience. Then we just talk to them, get to know them, and learn about their situation. This helps upper management keep the focus on the customer's needs. Afterward, if possible, it's also great to have that same customer meet with employees at each level of the organization—middle management and frontline workers.

Any place I've worked, we've also made it a point to send employees out to visit with customers. In the past, we've had frontline workers, managers, and executives go on ride-alongs with our salespeople. At Aviall, we sent out groups of frontline workers to meet with their counterparts at the airlines that buy our aircraft.

These in-person meetings provide specific, anecdotal data points about the company and its performance. They're great because they give a well-rounded picture of the impact a product makes. But they only tell the stories of a small fraction of the customers. As nice as it would be, in very large organizations it's impossible to speak to and meet directly with every single customer, which is why broader, more quantitative surveys still play a central role.

Conduct Useful Customer Surveys

Design a survey that communicates the true voice of the customer to employees, not just an aggregated number. Returning to the ice cream example, the company's customer relations team might have run surveys and told the production team something like "families love the product and the sundae flavors." Maybe those employees thought families would prefer a cheaper product, like a big ready-made sundae you could serve in scoops. This is pure speculation—I don't know what internal metrics led to the company discontinuing the product we loved—but this illustrates why specific feedback is important.

I chose its product because "my family loved its product," yes, but that's not the full story. We liked it *because* we could each have our own sundaes with our own flavors. That bit of insight could have helped the company innovate in a more intentional way.

This highlights a larger problem with most company surveying techniques: they don't go deep enough. The most common survey, the net promoter score, asks, "On a scale of 1 to 10, how likely are you to recommend this product/service to another person?"

If a customer would recommend, the answer is 10, if it wouldn't, it's 1. The net promoter score is how many advocates you have (9s or 10s) minus detractors (6 or less). That question gives you a great sense of company performance trends, but it doesn't tell you *why* you're doing well or what you're doing poorly. This kind of questioning alone cannot fuel sustainable growth. Each product has a host of features that you engineer into it, and you need to know exactly how those features add or subtract value, either practical or emotional, in the eyes of the customer.

The most important question to ask is, "Why do you choose us over our competitors?" From this, you can compile key data points that show which features your customers connect to. That way, when you change and innovate—as any company must—you make improvements *around* that core connection, improvements that will make the best parts of the product shine even brighter.

This is the path taken by almost every currently dominant technology company. Think about Google, Facebook, and Twitter. Each of these started with a core service—a platform for providing information, connecting people, and so on. Each innovation and update to their software has served to make the use of their technology more intuitive. The core product hardly changes, even as the companies expand and diversify their interests.

Once the customer's voice rings through your company halls, you need to make sure you keep that voice at the center during meetings and day-to-day operations. This requires a mindset shift—from a linear way of thinking to one that takes a 360-degree view of the customer.

Using a linear mindset, people approach problems in a predictable, straightforward way. "This is the problem, this is the goal. How do I get from point A to point B?" This inevitably leaves out important insights. For example, someone who seeks to solve a problem with fulfillment will rarely take into account the communication between the customer and the sales team or the customer and the marketing campaign. Without those considerations, an easy, obvious solution might be missed—for example, the sales team might be able to clarify expectations, or the marketing team might need to tweak its messaging to better target ideal customers.

When you craft a solution without considering all of the angles, it will likely fail to address the underlying problem and/

or it will break links in other parts of the chain. This is one of the ways that complexity accrues in a company—when employees develop their own, nonstandardized, siloed solutions, it often throws the rest of the company out of alignment and spawns even more unnecessary and highly individualized systems and solutions.

This isn't to say that you want your employees to avoid proactively solving problems—that's the whole point of this book. But they need to take that 360-degree view of both the situation and, most importantly, the customer. This is one of the things that whiteboard meetings are great for—they allow you to convene a team with diverse perspectives so the problem can be examined from every angle.

The other solution is to simplify. Make sure that everyone understands the key metrics and how to define success in each of them. For example, if the customer feedback surveys show that customers value quality, then you can clarify everyone's jobs and responsibilities by defining what high quality looks like at each step of the process—from product design to manufacturing, all the way through to fulfillment.

Look for Areas to Simplify

Once you've made sure that you can hear the customers' voice, you can let their needs and wants guide you in the hunt for areas to simplify. You'll find the best opportunities when you detangle three main loci of complexity:

- Points of friction
- Anchors
- Monuments

Reduce Points of Friction

Friction can arise at any point where a company interacts with customers. By friction, I mean anything that might negatively impact a customer's experience. To find unnecessary friction, start by mapping out the entire customer journey—from the first interaction through the entire sales cycle, delivery, and follow-up; be sure to include returns and refunds. For example, let's say that the first interaction comes when the customer orders a product online. Does the customer have to follow up with order status, or do you send status updates as you're fulfilling the order? Does the customer get a notice of when the order has shipped? Do they have the ability to track the package? Do they receive a notice when the product is delivered? Have they received information about the product's warranty? Is it clear how to use the product once it is received?

To reduce friction, make each step of the process as simple and intuitive for the customer as possible. Warranty claims are a great example. For a long time at Aviall, we shipped our warranty terms and conditions with the product, but we didn't post this information online. Humans often misplace things—even important things like tax returns. Less consequential items, like appliance warranties stand almost no chance. We regularly got calls from customers who couldn't find their warranty documents and had searched the web, but couldn't find them there. That was an unnecessary point of friction, so we posted the warranties online.

It should come as no surprise that the most successful companies in the twenty-first century are also the companies with the smoothest customer interface procedures. Part of this is likely due to their youth. The major innovations of the late twentieth and early twenty-first century all focused on simplifying the customer's life. Younger companies understand this. They recognize that any company that wants to compete *must* be a service company first. No one can rely on products alone.

Amazon is perhaps most responsible for this shift in customer expectations. It built an entire business around eliminating points of friction, offering ever faster and cheaper delivery on a massive selection of products. Amazon constantly innovates new ways to improve the customer experience, which makes it much harder for competing retailers to carve out a niche in the market.

Older companies still fall into the trap of thinking of themselves as product companies that don't have to worry about service. For example, many car dealerships think they sell cars, not experiences. This manifests in the countless little annoyances that come with buying a car, or getting your vehicle serviced. I once had to bring my car into the dealership to get something fixed three times in the same year, and each and every time, the mechanic came out and said, "Alright, we need you to fill out this intake form."

The intake form had all the same questions—name, date of birth, address, etc.—that I had already given the dealership, not only the first time I came into the shop for repairs, but years ago, *when I bought my car.* The whole time I filled out the paperwork, I felt my frustration rise as I thought, "There's no way they don't already have this on file."

What should have been a 30-second conversation with someone behind a computer turned into a 30-minute intake process. What's worse is that it happened even after I told them that I didn't have a lot of time. They said they'd make it go as quickly as possible, but then I waited three hours for the repairs, which didn't begin until after I'd completed the intake form. The final blow to their customer service rating came when they brought my car out. They said, "Usually, we wash it, but since you're in a rush, we didn't."

I know as well as anyone how long repairs can take, and I didn't expect them to boost me to the top of the queue or rush their work in order to get me out the door. But they certainly could have eliminated a couple of the more time-consuming steps of the repair process, including the intake, and I'm sure that they could have multitasked and cleaned my car while they serviced it or reset my expectation that it wouldn't be done ahead of time.

Contrast this experience with what happens when someone buys a vehicle from a younger company, like Tesla. A 2018 Experian survey found that Tesla had *the most loyal* customer base, with more than 80 percent of new Tesla owners/leasers deciding to buy or lease a Tesla as their next car. This customer retention mark trounced the next closest competitors—Ford and Subaru—by a full 8 percentage points.

Tesla owes part of this loyalty to the quality and novelty of its product, but a large part of this has to do with Tesla's customer service and how it reduces points of friction for customers. For one, the company controls every part of the customer experience. It doesn't contract sales out to multiple third-party dealers like other car companies do. This gives Tesla unprecedented levels of control over the buying and repair experience, and allows it to institute uniform high standards that have become synonymous with the brand. Tesla also invests in the customer experience *after* the point of purchase, including ongoing funding to construct a network of charging stations for Teslas and other electric vehicles with matching ports across the United States and Europe.

Some companies intentionally build points of friction into their operating processes in an attempt to boost profits. For example, a home improvement store might sell you an extended warranty, but then make the claims process so complicated that you cannot replace or get service for the malfunctioning product without spending hours on the phone being bounced around from department to department. This is one of the most egregious forms of short-term thinking imaginable. Best-case scenario, these intentional points of friction frustrate customers, driving them to the nearest competitor and damaging your bottom line. In the worst-case scenario, this kind of friction can prove fatal to the entire company.

Many people don't realize this, but Netflix didn't initially gain an advantage over Blockbuster because it was more efficient, but because it offered a reprieve from one key intentional friction point: late fees. During Netflix's early ascent, a significant share of Blockbuster's profits came from charging late fees, which amounted to penalizing patrons. At that time, before streaming, Blockbuster was the more efficient service with stores everywhere so you could grab a movie on your way home instead of waiting for it in the mail. Netflix, as a subscription-based service, allowed you to keep the DVDs for as long as you wanted without paying a late fee. That feature of its service pulled the first customers away from Blockbuster. Streaming was merely the coup de grâce.*

Cut Anchors

Anchors are old ways of operating or beliefs that restrict thinking. These shouldn't be confused with a founding purpose or core competitive advantage. In the case of Blockbuster, one point of friction (late fees) had become an anchor. Blockbuster's

---

* Greg Satell, "A Look Back at Why Blockbuster Really Failed and Why It Didn't Have To," *Forbes*, September 5, 2014, https://www.forbes.com/sites/gregsatell/2014/09/05/a-look-back-at-why-blockbuster-really-failed-and-why-it-didnt-have-to/?sh=42385a221d64.

CEO in the early aughts, John Antioco, realized that Netflix was crushing Blockbuster because of its late fees, so he got rid of them, a move that shrank revenue by $200 million. Some factions within Blockbuster leadership, still tethered to the old mindset, got nervous about the drop in revenue during already lean times, and argued that what they really needed to do was double down on what got the brand to its dominant position in the first place—late fees and brick-and-mortar retail stores. That faction got Antioco fired, and his replacement promptly reinstated late fees. The company was out of business in five years.

But that wasn't Blockbuster's only anchor, even if it was the one that dragged it to a full halt. The other was that it thought of itself as a source of community. Leadership believed that people came to video rental stores because of the interactions, the staff picks, the ritual of rental. Antioco had started investing in an online streaming service, Total Access. This service required loads of capital, and the recalcitrant factions within Blockbuster thought that it wasn't worth it because it pulled Blockbuster out of alignment with what they considered to be the core of their business—the community around the store.

Antioco recognized that a hybrid brick-and-mortar/streaming business model wouldn't compromise Blockbuster's purpose and that if the company didn't shift to streaming, it would fail in the information age. His successor couldn't see anything other than what had helped the company in the past. In the end, he made an inexcusably shortsighted decision, and steered his company to certain disaster.

Remove Monuments

Monuments are the physical testaments to anchors. They are the statues that companies build to pay homage to old ways of operating. To an outside observer, monuments usually look like trash, but the people in the organization feel a nostalgic attachment to them. Let's look at Blockbuster once more. Those brick-and-mortar stores became monuments. They represented what Blockbuster used to stand for—a type of community, the local workers who developed a face-to-face rapport with customers. It was a place where you could run into your neighbors and say hello or make a beeline to your favorite section with your kids, grab the newest release, and buy them some popcorn or candy, maybe even their favorite action figure. Blockbuster had this monument on such a high pedestal, its leadership couldn't see it being battered by outside forces until it came crashing down.

This is an extreme example—most companies don't have to detonate the very backbone of their operations to remove their monuments. Still, some monuments clutter up almost every company—stuff like old fax machines, poor broadband internet, even extra staplers—any remnant of times past that doesn't contribute to the flow of business. This sort of innocuous debris accumulates far faster than most people imagine, and it reduces both efficiency and employees' ability to innovate. Conversely, removing monuments greatly improves efficiency and inspires innovation.

For example, when I worked for Honeywell and went to Mexico to lead the Six Sigma revolution there, part of what we did was organize the factory floor. We made sure that everything had a specific place and that only the tools and equipment we still used remained on the floor. We did this throughout five factories, and freed up a *full quarter* of the floor space. This number shocked us. After streamlining the physical systems, we were able to improve the factories' output and efficiency, without paying for more space. This had cascading benefits. Because we could use our space better, we didn't have to open a new factory to meet increased demand. Not having to open a new factory simplified and reduced the cost of our supply chain, helped us avoid regulatory conundrums, and more. As a result, we were able to expand output, with much lower capital investment.

This had the secondary benefit of improving clarity across every aspect of the workflow. Everyone knew exactly what each machine and tool on the floor did and where it should be. Employees also knew how their jobs in the assembly line fit into the overall process. This is a form of radical transparency that improves the flow of information between employees. In doing so, employees were better able to make decisions and iterate their own processes. When processes are simplified, employees know how tasks are done and can understand the connections between departments. With that deeper understanding, they can make new connections and improvements.

Manage the Changes That Remove Complexity

Now that we've covered the three loci of complexity to look for and eliminate from your company, let's get into *how* to look for them and how to manage the change.

Use Swim Lane Diagrams

A great first step, something you can do tomorrow, is to create a swim lane diagram of each aspect of your company. I've used this tool to map out the processes within SUMMi7 to see where our handoffs are, where our costs come up, and what processes add unnecessary complexity. I also use it with clients, to help them map out processes across an entire company and projects within specific teams.

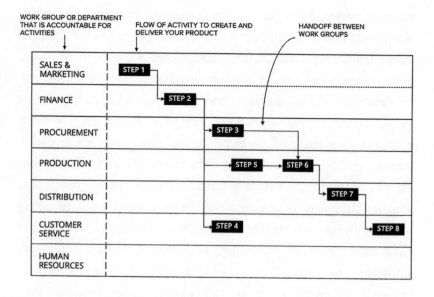

The diagram looks like an Olympic pool, where each worker in a team (or each department in an organization, depending on the scale) has a lane. In each worker's or department's lane, you list the responsibilities for each phase of the project, how much those actions will cost, and whether that cost is fixed or variable. Then you draw lines to indicate handoffs, either within the same lane or across lanes. As you work from left to right, it all flows and narrows until you end up with one product. Though they are not in the figure above, I like to add KPIs in each lane, so that employees know what their goals are and what success looks like for their teams. You end up with one diagram that shows the budget of each segment of the production process, for every individual or group involved, and how each one connects with the others.

With this visual element, you'll immediately see inefficiencies, waste, and pinch points, or the areas where teams end up waiting for one group before being able to move on. When you see the pinch points, you can either smooth out the production process by slowing all of the other lanes down, or you can redeploy resources to the lane that moves more slowly than the others to speed things up. This way, you can establish a clean operating rhythm that minimizes dead time for teams between tasks.

You also can look for opportunities to consolidate actions or handoffs. For example, if one document or piece of equipment gets handed back and forth between the marketing and the sales teams four or five times, look for ways to cut that down to two or three iterations while still maintaining the same commitment to quality.

Finally, this is a great tool that enables all employees in the company, from the upper levels of management to the frontline workers, to understand how what they do and what they're responsible for fits in with the rest of the organization. They know what's expected of them and when, and they can see easily how dropped balls interrupt everyone else's work. It bolsters accountability, and helps give frontline employees the bird's-eye view necessary to make transformative iterations to their own processes while maintaining alignment with the organization.

I've used this diagram to lead some of my most successful battles against complexity, most memorably in 2006, when I worked for Precision Conversions, a startup that converted 757 airplanes from passenger planes to cargo planes. With help from the other leaders, and leveraging the Six Sigma playbook, we mapped out the entire conversion process on a massive, 40-foot-long swim lane diagram we put on the wall of a large training room. We documented every activity, the inputs from one department and outputs to another, and the established goals that aligned each team. We then turned that diagram into a playbook of our entire operations. We aggregated all of the actions in each lane into a single chapter of the playbook.

Then we published the book on a drive shared with the entire firm, so everyone could see each team's responsibilities and work together to streamline those. This playbook served as our baseline, and whenever a proposed change in operations came up, everyone could check it against the playbook to make sure that it wouldn't create any inadvertent complexities or inefficiencies. This way, we managed to head off new process problems before they arose, and we had a clear understanding of where we stood, which allowed us to leap forward with greater conviction.

Once you've used a swim lane diagram to identify areas you want to change, you have to make those changes to reduce complexity. Convincing people to change with you is one of the greatest challenges in business. There are countless clichés about why people avoid change: because they fear the unknown, because they're comfortable, because change carries risks. All of these, on a certain level, are true. But they are mere symptoms of a much deeper anxiety, the root fear that keeps most people stuck—fear of not being in control, and more specifically, not being as effective at your job once the change is implemented. Most people spend years mastering their craft, and change can send them back to the starting line.

So many people, especially frontline employees and middle managers, resist change because they fear that they'll be excluded and will lose their place in shaping their own future, so they struggle to visualize what change will look like for them. Left unaddressed, this anxiety will hamstring any effort to streamline procedures. Years of companies' myopic focus on profits has made employees skeptical of simplification initiatives. Some might think their jobs will disappear if the company finds a way to remove too many steps. For a simplification effort to work, each employee needs to buy into it and bring his or her own unique contributions and insights. If the company leaders can manage change effectively, they will empower their employees to participate and even lead the change. Employees will view the simplification effort less as a seismic shift to be wary of and more as an opportunity to make their lives easier and more rewarding.

There are two attitudes that leaders can instill in their workforces to create this outcome:

- A feeling of gratitude
- A growth mindset with a future orientation

A Feeling of Gratitude

I believe that in order to give anything, you must be grateful for what you have. This holds true for individuals and organizations. When you are grateful for what you have, for your strengths and your accomplishments, you recognize what you have. When you know what you have, then you can share it freely. This has three implications: First, it means that managers need to practice gratitude themselves before they can lead anybody else. Second, it means that they need to lead their employees and coworkers in practicing gratitude as well. And third, it means that when leading a change effort, managers must acknowledge the workers' (and the company's) achievements, both past and present.

Starting at the personal level, as a leader, you need to celebrate where you are. If your entire mindset is, "I'm not good enough. I haven't done enough," then all of the people you're leading will feel belittled. They'll assume that you're judging them because you've made it further than they have, and you're so hard on yourself. This doesn't mean that you should get complacent—you just need to be gentle with yourself as you grow. Gratitude makes this gentleness possible. Not only will it help you connect with your employees, it will fuel your own growth. For example, in 2018, I decided that something I needed to work on was showing more vulnerability at work. For a while after making this commitment, I felt uncomfortable. I took a few steps back and reflected on *why* I was so buttoned up. It came from growing up in a household where I had to be strong and self-sufficient at a young age. I needed to take care of my friends and family, and put on a calm, stoic demeanor to do it. My discomfort with vulnerability came from this impulse. But my ability to be stoic and self-sufficient had helped me in my career, so I had to acknowledge how far this past version of myself had gotten me. I also had to consciously choose to be open and vulnerable. After all of that, I started to make progress, but it still takes work.

Humans often mirror behaviors and mindsets that they see around them—it's why yawns are contagious. The same thing holds true for a mindset of gratitude. Leaders who really embrace gratitude and use it to authentically engage with their employees will spread the mindset of gratitude throughout their entire team, almost without trying.

Finally, the starting point of any change process has to be gratitude. Whenever I'm leading a meeting to discuss a new initiative, I give an overview of how we got to where we are, how the old system served us well, and how much we as a company or a team have achieved. This basis in gratitude shifts the entire focus of the meeting. That way, when we discuss a new initiative, it's not as a Band-Aid or as a response to a crisis but as an opportunity to achieve more. This positive framing will always inspire more lasting engagement than negative messaging. Often and *especially* in periods of crisis, like when a company faces bankruptcy, managers lead with a message of fear instead of gratitude. They think that they need to make employees understand that if they don't work hard, they will get fired. As hard as it can be, this is the moment when you need to focus on gratitude the *most*. Instead of outlining how poor of a position the company is in, put focus on what you can control, where you will go, and the advantages you have. If you're going to save the company, you need people to believe that it can be saved.

A Growth Mindset with a Future Orientation

According to Stanford psychologist Carol Dweck, most people have either a fixed mindset or a growth mindset. People with a fixed mindset believe that they are who they will always be. This mindset makes any sort of institutional change nearly impossible. On the other hand, people with a growth mindset believe that they can develop and that change is possible. This is the mindset you need to instill in your workforce to lead change, and you need to pair it with the proper orientation.

Everyone has a tendency to orient personal thinking either toward the past or the future. People with an orientation toward the past find energy and inspiration in legacies and histories. They feel a deep connection to old accomplishments, draw pride from them, and look to the past to develop new solutions. People with a future orientation spend their time planning. They draw inspiration from possibilities and groundbreaking ideas. I happen to be oriented toward the future—I'm always imagining the next step, looking around the corner, excited to discover or explore something new. There's nothing inherently good or bad about either orientation, and to be successful, most companies need a healthy mix of both. Being too focused on the future can make you lose sight of what made your company unique and profitable in the first place. As I mentioned in Chapter 2, going back and revitalizing your connection to the company's founding purpose can serve as a profound guide to your future options.

Effective change management requires a combination of future orientation and a growth mindset. Fortunately, both can be instilled with the same key strategies. Managers need to paint a compelling vision of the future to inspire people to undergo the necessary shifts. I frequently revisit this in meetings immediately after I outline the company's current position and celebrate what we've accomplished. You won't be surprised to know that I use a whiteboard, which I divide into two sections: our present and our future. I draw contrasts between the two, showing what the negative effects of continuing down our current path might be and how much we all stand to gain by making changes.

For someone to feel truly excited about the future, that person must have the ability to shape it. In these meetings, when I'm writing out the vision for the future, I may start with my own goals and the company's goals. But then I ask employees to contribute, with questions like: "What kind of company would we have to be for you to wake up every day excited to go to work?" "What would have to be true for customers to choose us over our competitors?" "What can we do to make sure that our products or our services make a greater impact in the world?"

In doing this, we collaborate on a vision of the future, one that employees feel ownership of and are motivated to achieve. Once we have the vision, the aspiration, we can plan how to get there from where we are now. The first step is the hardest, so I make sure to draw on the board the very first thing that everyone in the room can do, and I challenge each person to accomplish it the next day. And then we are on our way.

8

PARTNER TO ADVANCE TOGETHER

Once you've made frontline leadership the norm, you'll have an agile, innovative, aligned company, composed of purposeful and inclusive leaders at every level. This presents a new and exciting opportunity. You can leverage all of those empowered employees to enter into even greater, mutually rewarding partnerships, especially with two of the key partners introduced in Chapter 2, your customers and your community. I've reserved this last chapter to take a deeper dive into partnering with these groups because the strength of your partnerships with them will determine both your competitive advantage and the overall impact your company can make. Managed correctly, these partnerships can become your company's greatest competitive advantage. If neglected, they can prove ruinous.

Partner with Customers

The true indicator of sustainable success in the turbulent twenty-first century is not how well a company navigates change but how well it helps its *customers* navigate change. Customers don't need vendors—they need partners. Consider that the uncertainty and discomfort evolving technology creates for your internal operations also causes the same uncertainty and discomfort for your customers. And one of the greatest fears behind uncertainty is the idea of having to face it alone.

Imagine what would be possible if you begin to think of your customers as partners. What would be possible if, together, you survey the landscape, collaborate to identify their key needs, and then move forward in lockstep. Not only can you close any gaps in service, you can prevent new gaps from opening—gaps that otherwise could be exploited by a lithe and lean startup.

A good example of this is, while leading Aviall, I attended an industry air show where customers, suppliers, and other industry partners met to discuss current and future concerns and opportunities. We had just completed a major IT systems upgrade, and we were still transitioning to a new set of processes. I had a couple of meetings with customers to discuss their current needs and future opportunities, but the only thing everyone wanted to talk about was how much of a headache Aviall's new processes had become. While the IT upgrade was essential, we hadn't leveraged our existing partnerships with our customers well enough to ensure that our change didn't impact their operations. Had we put in place a stronger, more proactive partnership, we could have collaborated with our customers, refining processes and testing with them throughout the design and implementation of the new system, minimizing their inconvenience. That was a long year. Although our business declined somewhat, we didn't lose any customers in the long run and recovered the next year. We managed, but it was the exact kind of gap that an opportunistic competitor could have used to lure out customers away.

Strong partnerships with customers depend on two keys:

- Connecting customer insights to action
- Adapting to change together

Connecting Customer Insights to Action

In the first seven or eight years of my career, at Pratt & Whitney and at Honeywell, I experienced firsthand how difficult it can be for a frontline employee to foster an open and ongoing dialogue with customers. When I worked in back-office operations, I was rarely exposed to customers. Those of us in the back office relied on the front-facing departments, like sales and customer service, for feedback. But it took months to get information from customers through the sales team to us, and even then, it wasn't a dialogue. We received survey results or anecdotal information filtered through a single person's lens, which meant we never had a chance to ask follow-up questions or gain a deeper understanding firsthand.

To be able to innovate, solve problems, and provide better solutions to the customers identified, I needed to actually know what they thought. We all did. Of course, connecting each employee to each customer is a complicated, if not impossible, task. The best way to do this efficiently is to simplify communication as much as possible by looking for any overlap in customer concerns that may point to a process issue that you can address by sharing insights with teams engaged in that process. The next step is to encourage deeper employee-customer connections.

Look for Overlap in Customer Concerns

At Honeywell, many of our customers expressed concern over the same key issues. A major one was that they struggled to keep track of the shifting international regulatory environment. Armed with this knowledge, we created a group to monitor new regulations that would affect the industry. Whenever we detected a shift, we informed our customers *and* offered a well-thought-out solution to any issues the new regulation might cause. In doing so, we saved our customers resources that would have gone toward looking for a solution we had already identified. This also served to further communication with all our customers, which we used as a foundation to obtain greater one-on-one engagement and create specialized initiatives.

It is important to note that in my experience, the vast majority of customer complaints can be traced, not to a failure from one specific employee but to a gap or breakdown in processes. This was obviously the case in this example, as we didn't have a mechanism in place to track regulatory changes. Even so, in the old top-down model, some managers might have had the inclination to find someone to blame for this lack of communication, maybe getting frustrated that their customer-facing employees weren't taking the initiative to research the regulations and share the findings with our customers. Those managers might believe that demanding such a degree of foresight raises expectations and performance from employees.

While this logic seems compelling, it often does more harm than good. High performance comes from a combination of high expectations and support, not high expectations and blame. Fault-finding prevents an open, inclusive, and trusting environment. For this reason, I always first look for a process improvement that can resolve a customer issue, before blaming a team member, even in situations where it seems like someone clearly dropped the ball. Often, that localized mistake is a symptom of a larger operational disease.

Encourage Deeper Employee–Customer Connections

For a large company to respond to the voice of the customer, it must cover as many gaps in customer relationships as possible. The best people to fill those gaps are the ones who are in the best position to see them: frontline leaders. Encourage every employee to connect with customers, and lead by example, by making sure you spend time with customers every week. Then support your employees' efforts with a robust baseline program that connects employees at each level of the organization to the customer, using tools like customer spotlights—during which a customer comes to speak with the executive team and tour a facility—and pointed, topic-specific surveys to shed light on why a customer chooses you over a competitor. That said, even the best customer relationship management system will have gaps. But if you have a cohort of frontline leaders who hold the expectation that everyone will focus on the voice of the customer, they will find novel ways to engage without guidance from above.

One powerful example comes from my time at Aviall. A role model for fronline leadership named J.R. Hoffman noticed that the employees on his team responsible for quality assurance had never seen a customer in action. So Hoffman booked a bus to take 20 employees to an aircraft maintenance, repair, and overhaul shop. There, the employees met the people who worked on the planes and helicopters that used Aviall's parts. They got to see the aircraft in action. They heard about times these aircraft had been used to evacuate people during a hurricane and to deliver relief during floods. One aircraft out of commission could mean lives lost. That meeting did more than open a dialogue between the people who use our products and the people who supply them, as each employee left inspired to improve his or her performance and find new ways to innovate.

A key note that underscores the importance of empowering your employees, Hoffman didn't bring this program up with the executive team until *after* the first test. When he did, we loved it, and gave all the support we could to expand it. Hoffman now runs Customer Connect, a large, companywide project that brings employees to the field to interact with customers. His initiative changed how the entire company operates, and it only happened because he had the freedom to execute it. In the old model of top-down leadership, Hoffman might have been punished for executing his plan without prior approval, or may have lost time trying (and even failing) to sell it to upper management before implementation. He only felt comfortable doing what he did because he knew that even if he failed, we would have appreciated his effort because it aligned directly with our purpose and values—focusing on customers and investing in our employees.

To help programs like this be effective, make sure your employees know *how* to communicate and engage. Two pillars foundational to successful partnerships that employees can build their communication strategies on are:

- Practicing empathy
- Aligning expectations

Practicing Empathy

The most advanced customer relations processes are useless if you fail to listen to what customers say and to empathize with their experience. On the other hand, doing so will help you respond to their needs and allow you to build meaningful partnerships. For instance, at Honeywell, a recently hired senior leader at one of our customers stopped by to establish a relationship. He skipped the pleasantries and launched into a list of problems that his company had with us. Rather than become defensive, I sat and listened, for nearly an hour. When he finished, I told him that I needed to go into the back office to get some data and gain some perspective on what he was talking about. He was so agitated that he followed me, repeating his complaints the whole time.

I finally helped him calm down enough to take a couple of steps back and establish a dialogue. I saw right away that he was operating under immense pressure. During our dialogue it became clear that his stress was compounded by the fact that his boss had sent him to Honeywell without a specific goal in mind, only to get some sort of general improvement from us. Initially, he'd responded to all of this uncertainty by attacking perceived issues, but as we talked, we were able to identify a couple of specific areas where we could improve, and I promised him results. This was the start of a fruitful partnership, but it never would have happened if I hadn't taken the time to ask questions, listen deeply to his replies, and empathize with his situation.

Listening and empathy should be the guiding principles of all communication with customers, and if company leadership sets that expectation and models that behavior, then everyone else will follow. A good place to start is with an exercise popularized by Amazon CEO Jeff Bezos, who includes an empty chair in each meeting to represent the customer. Here are a few other ideas: start or end meetings with a quote from a customer, post pictures or videos of customers in action at your facilities, and bring customers in to share at your town hall meetings. The more you can help your employees see customers and listen to their real experiences, needs, and concerns, the easier it will be to build empathy and connection and reinforce your purpose as a company.

Aligning Expectations

Trust and transparency buttress any successful dialogue, and one of the best ways to develop both is to make sure that your customers' expectations are aligned with the services you provide. This came up frequently during my time at Honeywell. For example, we had an instance when our customers had a different definition of success than we did regarding delivery of our products to their warehouses. We measured an order being fulfilled when it shipped from *our* dock, but customers measured order fulfillment based on when it arrived at *their* docks. That disconnect caused customers to believe that we'd failed to fulfill their orders on time, while we saw the same information and thought the opposite. When we looked at the numbers, it appeared to us that we'd filled 99 percent of our orders on time, while customers looked at the same numbers and thought only 60 percent had been fulfilled on time.

The solution was to develop an understanding of the disconnect, agree on a scorecard we both would use to track and share performance, and plan a transition to the new process that required change from both teams. Once we did this, we shared information monthly to validate our performance and address any issues. As we closed the performance gap, we used those monthly meetings to discuss other improvements we could make in our service. This is a great example of how collaborating with a customer on one issue can spill over to other process improvements and open new growth opportunities.

Sometimes, a company's track record of excellence can set the bar so impossibly high that it throws all expectations out of alignment. For example, at Aviall, we went through a period of relatively slow business. As a result, during that period we filled our orders in half the usual time required. When business picked up, our deliveries returned to the previous turnaround times.

Some customers perceived this as a drop in performance, even though we'd met the terms of the contract. Since customers had become accustomed to the faster speed, they had adjusted their expectations accordingly and started to rebuild their own processes around them. This, obviously, upset some of our customers and jeopardized our partnership and our ability to work together. Once we explained to them that the elevated service that they'd received was the result of doing our best to overdeliver whenever possible, but that their expectations should remain at the standard of service we'd agreed to in our terms, we were able to reset expectations and rebuild the relationships. It is this sort of communication that provides the degree of trust necessary to create an open, fruitful dialogue and partnership with your customers.

Adapt to Change Together

Once you've established a strong dialogue with your customers and empowered your frontline leaders, you can enter into a deeper level of partnership by codeveloping innovation with your customers. In the traditional, or "waterfall," method of developing new products or technology, a company gathers information, takes the requirements into a backroom, and unilaterally develops a solution over several months or years. Although that may have worked in the past, the pace of change today renders that process irrelevant. With customer codevelopment, you work with your customers from the outset to develop new solutions and improved responses to the issues that they face.

At Aviall, we did this by creating a codevelopment lab called Innovation Applied. We invited our customers to come, share their concerns, and then give us input on the best way to solve these issues. We then developed a proof of concept and brought our early work back to the customers for feedback. By incorporating the customers into the iterative process, we were able to deliver more value while minimizing rework and ensuring that whatever solution we landed on would still serve their needs.

To expand upon an earlier example, the software we developed at Aviall to track the storage and handling information for the chemicals involved in airplane maintenance (discussed in Chapter 6) went through our Innovation Applied Lab. We asked several airlines to explain how they used and tracked chemicals, what their biggest pain points were, and what sort of software solution would help them the most. Then we used the expertise of our frontline employees to populate the software with all the relevant information about the chemicals and shape a solution that met our customers' most important needs. This is customer codevelopment—combining our frontline workers' knowledge with our customers' know-how to develop an elegant, simple solution to a complex problem.

A remarkable aspect of this project was that it brought together *direct competitors* in the industry. They all had the same problem—handling chemicals—and we encouraged them to work together and brainstorm solutions with us. They were willing to do so because none of these airlines differentiated themselves in the market by how they handled chemicals. Of course, there are still many conversations that are best managed one-on-one with a customer. But when you can get multiple perspectives from the same industry, then you can develop truly comprehensive, collaborative solutions.

Communicating directly with customers in this way can help you develop better, smarter products and stay ahead of market shifts. But it offers other benefits: because we went to such lengths to provide more value to our customers, they returned the favor. The customers who participated in the Innovation Applied Lab became advocates for our company and our approach to serving them. They told their peers about their experience with us and the work we'd done to tailor our offerings to their needs. We'd acted as an extension of their organization, and, in turn, they acted as an extension of ours. Through this, we both grew, despite changes and challenges within our industries. That's the power of partnership.

Partner with Communities

I grew up in the small, blue-collar town of Brockport, New York. My mom worked as a receptionist at a doctor's office, and my dad was a union electrical worker. We knew everybody in my neighborhood. Many came to the doctor my mom worked for, had kids I went to school with, and shopped at the same stores. Every weekend, my parents helped neighbors with whatever project they were working on, whether it was cutting down trees or repairing a light in their house. The kids would run around the neighborhood, more or less given free rein, because every other parent in the community knew who we were and were looking out for us.

Yet in the twenty-first century, those tight-knit communities are fewer and harder to find. While a myriad of factors have contributed to the dissolution of American communities, most companies can address one major factor: the tilt toward a myopic focus on shareholder value. This focus has led companies to strip community engagement programs from their budgets. But those programs provide vital support to almost everyone who comes into contact with the company. They make communities stronger and more resilient, and, more often than not, those community engagement programs even pay dividends.

Beyond that, everyone (including every organization) has a moral obligation to make our world a better place. I wrote this book in the summer of 2020, a transformative time for me. I took a voluntary furlough during the COVID-19 crisis. That furlough gave me something I don't think I've had since college, if ever: two uninterrupted weeks to just think, read, and reflect. During those two weeks, the protests in the wake of the killing of George Floyd started, and that year's great reckoning with racism in America broke out.

It was a turbulent time, but also a hopeful one. The country engaged in a lot of amazing, constructive dialogue. It inspired me to reflect on what I love most about this America—the promise that people have the freedom to improve their situation. Yet, in many ways, we have failed to live up to that golden promise, especially to the Black community, but also to many others. Several communities, and the people within them, face unfair and often insurmountable barriers. Contemplating all this, I thought back to the community I grew up in, with its powerful and wide-ranging support system. I searched for ways to make a tangible, positive impact in the world. And that's how I landed on this idea: we must partner with and invest in our communities as the fundamental building block of a strong society. It is the only way to truly build a culture of inclusion and to confront the challenges we face. In short, companies need to leverage their resources—their money, their influence, and especially their frontline leaders—to become community leaders.

A community leader is a person or an organization that recognizes that the strength of our country comes from its diversity. A community leader doesn't operate through hierarchies or dicta, but lets the needs and voices of the community lead the way. Thus, to foster effective partnerships with communities, your company needs to focus on two priorities:

- Be transparent about what you stand for beyond the walls of your company.
- Invest in communities to promote the common good.

Be Transparent About What Your Company Stands For

Millennials and "zoomers" (members of Generation Z) care far more than previous generations did about making an impact on issues that matter to them. This might have something to do with the fact that they grew up with the internet and had access to boundless information about the inequalities in the world. This also might be because so many of the problems we face—climate change, lack of sustainability, deteriorating infrastructure—will affect them the most. These generations know well the ills of the world, and they want to do their part to fix them. Even though we've made significant improvements in many areas, such as reducing poverty and improving health, there's more information and visibility than ever before on the significant opportunity in front of us to do more. Because of all this, if a company wants to attract and retain top young talent, it must emphasize what it stands for by operating in complete alignment with its values. It must prioritize working to make a positive impact, not just to its bottom line but to the world.

The days where the ends (even the best-intentioned ones) justified the means are over. To demonstrate what you stand for through action, you must:

- Put social issues on the agenda.
- Empower your employees to partner with communities.
- Organize companywide engagement to take meaningful, measurable action.

Put Social Issues on the Agenda

In the aftermath of the 2020 wave of Black Lives Matter protests, several large companies released statements and ads touting their commitment to social justice. While these statements represented a great first step, raised awareness, and showed solidarity, they alone do little to change the material reality of disadvantaged populations. To publish an ad and not back it up with action will only hurt a company's image over time. For a company to truly align with its values, it needs to work toward real change. Not only will this make a positive impact, it will also foster goodwill and trust—with customers and the general public. On the other hand, the public will hold companies accountable for any failure to live up to their stated ideals.

One simple, yet profound, change that you can make to ensure that your company puts its values into action and strives toward real progress is to add social impact to whatever scorecard or framework you use to evaluate success. I did that when I founded SUMMi7, by adding social impact to a framework we use called the balanced scorecard. This is the method that guides our entire agenda. It's how we set goals, how we develop our long-term strategy, and how we decide what our next move will be. With social impact now on our scorecard, we consider every potential decision through the lens of how it will impact the community. We can avoid choices that might do harm, and steer toward partnerships, decisions, and investments that will improve overall quality of life. And, because we discuss our scorecard in nearly every meeting, our social impact is now part of our daily conversations. This constant focus has a multiplier effect on the amount of good we can do, as we continuously think of new ways to make a difference.

Empower Employees to Build Community Partnerships

The engaged, passionate workers of the twenty-first century can act as potent agents of change. All the company has to do is support them. One of the most effective ways to do this is to provide the infrastructure and funding to affinity/interest groups that employees can use to coordinate action, both internally and externally. At Aviall, we had affinity groups for Black, Asian American, and LGBTQ+ communities, among others. Many of my colleagues cited these groups as their most cherished sources of support and as the conduits that helped them contribute the most to society. This makes sense—each affinity group celebrates a specific part of an employee's identity, and gives that employee an outlet to engage in meaningful work within those communities. With this support, people feel comfortable showing up in a more authentic way. They don't feel like they need to hide aspects of their identity. They understand that the company they work for cares about the same communities they do. Few things fuel performance as much as a sense of belonging and the freedom to show up authentically, and there are few motivators more powerful than a deep connection to purpose and meaning.

These affinity groups also support an inclusive atmosphere. The Black affinity group isn't just open to Black employees, nor is the LGBTQ+ group open only to LGBTQ+ employees. Each of these groups welcomes members from any background. This fosters deeper understanding among an entire workforce. People come together to learn about the unique challenges facing specific groups and support their coworkers with their advocacy. Simple engagement on this level has tremendous power. The most virulent prejudice comes from an inability to empathize with other people. Programs like these break down the barriers that keep people ignorant of other cultures' perspectives and challenges.

It might seem like a small thing—having lunches with employees from different backgrounds or a few community service projects—but it adds up. Millions of people work for Fortune 1000 companies. If we can turn our workplaces into spaces that promote diversity, equity, inclusion, and understanding, it will go a long way toward building a society that lives up to the promise of freedom for all.

The positive impact of affinity groups within your organization can be multiplied when you bring these diverse perspectives together to work on a specific issue. In my opinion, the best way to solve the major problems in the twenty-first century is through intercommunity coalitions. The most pressing problems are also the most complex—requiring more imaginative and large-scale solutions and coordinated efforts across many different countries. For example, global warming cannot be tackled without a coalition of major international stakeholders. That sort of macro-level coalition building is the final frontier of leadership, and it's dizzyingly complicated. But it will also never be successful without micro-level efforts to foster understanding among diverse groups so that we can attack problems together.

Not only do these affinity groups improve the net social impact of the company, they do it in the most effective way possible. Employees and frontline workers are embedded in their communities, so they often have a direct connection to the problems they're trying to solve, and they're the best people to empower to develop a solution.

During my time at Aviall, this sort of frontline engagement made up the vast majority of our community programs. Many of our frontline managers regularly coordinated half days on Fridays, when everyone pushed to finish their work in the morning so that the team could volunteer at a food shelter or some other organization in the afternoon. One of my favorite parts about that company was just how prevalent these community initiatives were and how little I knew about what was happening. Because frontline managers had the power to undertake initiatives on their own, they rarely asked for permission. I take great satisfaction in knowing that I never heard about 90 percent of the community service that Aviall employees organized. To me, this demonstrates frontline leadership at its best.

Of course, we had this large organization, and all employees faced their own unique challenges in life. They often enlisted their coworkers to make a difference in an area that impacted them or their loved ones. One powerful example was our commitment to the juvenile diabetes walks at Aviall. Beyond that, we participated in fundraisers for the American Cancer Society and for organizations that support people with Down syndrome, ALS, heart disease, and others. This helped us make a big impact. We raised a lot of money for important causes and improved the lives of thousands of people. But it also helped us foster a strong community within our company. It allowed employees who struggled with a specific challenge to show up authentically, to not feel like they needed to hide a major aspect of their lives, and to feel the love and support of all of their teammates when they needed it most.

Organize Companywide Engagement in the Community

A self-organizing workforce does not exempt organizations from developing their own community engagement initiatives. Not doing so would be an abdication of leadership. Organizations are members of a community, too, and they should invest in those communities with their own macro-level initiatives. That said, as a senior leader, you can take community engagement cues from your employees. At Aviall, I was part of a legacy of leaders that made sure to organize large companywide events, and if I felt like we needed to branch out, I would ask other leaders in the organization what they were doing to make a difference and then look for ways to scale that.

I also took inspiration for these projects from our company's values. For example, since the founder of Aviall had served in the military, one of our values was supporting our veterans. These people have made tremendous sacrifices to serve our nation, and all too often, either because of physical or psychiatric injuries, they often struggle to support themselves. We wanted to help, so we partnered with the Adaptive Training Foundation, which provides free physical training to veterans and others with life-altering physical injuries. The programs go beyond functional rehabilitation, helping participants train for specific sports. This enables people to rediscover a connection with their body as a powerful, amazing, and special aspect of who they are. It might seem inconsequential, but this kind of intense, disciplined training also can facilitate the healing of the mental scars that accompany life-altering injuries.

No one who works for Aviall has expertise in how to offer this kind of training, but we wanted to help as many people as possible, so we offered financial support to this organization. Then to foster a deeper level of partnership, several of us regularly went to the gym and worked out with the veterans. We got to know them, hear their stories, and empathize. We never focused on their disabilities, pitied them, or went on these tours to congratulate ourselves for our financial contributions. We were just a group of athletes, sweating through our workouts, together.

Invest in Communities

The partnerships I've described are great for targeted action to respond to a specific problem. But companies also can have a lasting impact at scale, by partnering with and investing in major community pillars, such as education and small businesses. These kinds of investments help develop individuals and entities that will pay it forward and strengthen communities and economies for generations to come.

Invest in Education

Any company serious about making a positive change in its communities must support the schools in those communities at multiple levels of education. Several large companies, especially those in the science, technology, engineering, and math (STEM) fields, already do this. For example, Amazon partners with schools in the Pacific Northwest, providing equipment and expertise to make computer science classes available to youth from disadvantaged backgrounds.

These programs, while expensive, always pay dividends in the long run. Most school teachers and university professors don't get exposed to the latest research and technology and how it's being applied in the business world. But companies like Amazon can help bring this knowledge along with supporting tools and techniques into the classroom to help prepare the next generation to successfully engage in the workforce.

As companies grow, they will need to hire new employees. Yet most students entering the workforce will have been trained by people without knowledge of recent industry trends, a problem that will only get worse as technological innovation accelerates. When those students enter the workforce, they might only know how to use four- or five-year-old technology, which means their knowledge will be outdated, and they will have to be taught how to use contemporary systems on the job, if they can get jobs at all. By partnering with schools to codevelop curricula, companies can ensure that graduating students will be competitive applicants, which provides a better labor pool from which to recruit.

This is only a secondary benefit. The primary benefit of these partnerships runs much deeper—raising the bar for what children believe they can accomplish. This alone fosters a profound shift. If you grow up in an area where most people work minimum-wage jobs, generally, that's what you'll expect from life. But programs, like the ones run by Amazon, not only introduce kids to new career opportunities, they also show that someone believes in their ability to achieve. To really hammer home this belief, both companies go out of their way to connect directly with the students. Jeff Bezos has made visits to classrooms that received support from Amazon.

In the twenty-first century, supporting people in a way that raises the bar is more important than ever. Since outcomes in the contemporary American economy can often be underwhelming, especially for those from disadvantaged backgrounds, the tendency is to lower expectations. With more people carrying minimum-wage jobs into later stages in life, we talk about raising the minimum wage. This isn't to say we shouldn't raise the minimum wage. We absolutely should. But the focus can't just be on that one solution. We need to invest in communities in a way that ensures that people won't have to rely on minimum-wage jobs to support their families.

Invest in Small Businesses

Entrepreneurs and small businesses are integral parts of the fabric of any community. Beyond providing jobs, they give each small town, neighborhood, and street corner its unique flavor. Small coffee shops and restaurants provide places for people to gather and connect around local topics and events. Small business owners and entrepreneurs become role models and leaders in a community, especially in disadvantaged areas. They have the opportunity to expand the image of what is possible for children, become powerful voices on policy, and help their neighbors grow and succeed.

After I left Boeing, I transitioned to working full-time at SUMMi7. Our mission is to support small and medium-sized businesses, especially those owned by women, people of color, and veterans, by leveraging our experience to help them grow In order to live up to this purpose, we need to include voices from the communities we want to serve. I also wanted to build a team that is diverse in every sense of the word, from race and gender to experience, size of company, and functional expertise. Our goal is to bring our diverse experiences together and combine them into a program to help others. We want to move the needle, to foster economic opportunity and equality. To do that, we had to make a major commitment. In an early meeting with the founding team, we decided that at least half of the companies we work with will be owned by women, people of color, and veterans, and that the people we hire will reflect the businesses we're committed to supporting. Having a diverse team that is actively inclusive will enable us to benefit from the varied perspectives our team can bring to the issues these businesses face.

This journey has enabled me to meet many business leaders who partner with entrepreneurs to make a positive impact in their communities. Foremost among them are Jenny Poon and Odeen Domingo, cofounders of a Phoenix, Arizona, coworking space called CO+HOOTS. This is a purpose-driven organization focused on creating a flexible, supportive, inclusive ecosystem for entrepreneurs and small businesses. Independent from her work with CO+HOOTS, Jenny does creative design, and she joined the founding SUMMi7 team as our product design lead. As we worked together, we connected over our shared purpose and passion—supporting new companies, improving racial equality, and providing economic opportunity. At CO+HOOTS she had this workspace and this community of businesses, and I had a program designed for the same community that she served, so we decided to collaborate. CO+HOOTS partners with several local organizations, including the City of Mesa, Arizona.

In 2020, the city launched the Mesa CARES program to support the community in the wake of the coronavirus pandemic. Through this program, CO+HOOTS received funding to host a series of free webinars for local small business owners, and Jenny brought me in as one of the speakers. I delivered a presentation on how businesses can adapt to the new normal, and also donated several coaching calls to help small business owners stay focused on their purpose and survive the economic downturn.

I did this because I know how important small businesses are to the strength of a community. But it also helps me understand the unique problems that entrepreneurs face, which, in turn, helps inform the programs we offer at SUMMi7.

You don't have to step outside of the corporate culture to support small businesses in your community. Large companies can and should do this as well. The Unilever Sustainable Living Plan (USLP) is a great example of this sort of partnership. This plan, with a core aim to create a sustainable business, encompasses several initiatives and goals that target a few key areas of growth. One of the most important is a massive effort to support small businesses in underserved parts of the world to help them grow and scale. Unilever leverages its technology, product, marketing, and financial expertise to help 1.8 million entrepreneurs in their network (mom-and-pop shops, micro-retailers, street vendors, etc.) around the world who sell Unilever products. One of their simplest and most successful programs focuses on helping small and rural retailers digitize their systems. Simply switching from cash-only sales and analog inventory to digital sales and bookkeeping helps retailers obtain data on which products sell best and at what price, enabling those retailers to better manage inventory. Beyond that, having verifiable, digital records improves their access to small business loans, as they are able to prove their ability to repay, and greater capital to spur further growth.

Through this program and others like it, Unilever not only provides economic opportunity to their partners, reducing income inequality and empowering women and other marginalized groups, it also creates partnerships that help Unilever brands reach the more than 3 billion people living in rural areas in emerging markets.

For large companies, investments like this might appear as no more than a blip on their balance sheets. But they can make a world of difference for local businesses, and breathe new life into a community.

All of these transformations must start with one individual making a choice. As I've written this book, I've noticed my own personal purpose changing and growing. Having arrived at the end of these pages, I've landed on a new articulation: my purpose is to help create opportunities for others. To me, this is one of the most fundamental and vital goals of leadership. But it isn't the only way to define leadership, or the only way you can serve.

As we bring this conversation to a close, I invite you to reflect and consider: What's your purpose right now? How can you leverage your strengths to make a difference in the world? In your community? In your family? Once you have the answer, pursue it with your whole being.

EPILOGUE

Working with dozens of startups and entrepreneurs through the years, I often see potential in people (and their companies) who have yet to believe in themselves. I have the benefit of objectivity, natural optimism, and faith in people and in the future. I know that everybody has tremendous potential, and that everyone who desires it can develop into a unique, powerful leader—provided he or she receives the right support, guidance, and mentorship. I was lucky to have mentors and support as I developed in my career, and I know that too many are not as fortunate.

I hope that we can create a world where people see their strengths, know what energizes them, are able to be authentic to themselves and others, and understand that those qualities are enough to make a meaningful contribution to whatever field they choose to pursue. I hope that this book has provided some guidance, to help you discover your own strengths, as well as enable others to make their meaningful contributions. If you follow the guidance in these pages, and work with diligence and creativity, then you will likely find some version of success—as an individual and as a leader.

You can seize all the opportunities of frontline leadership if you stay humble. All you need to remember is that everything you do is for a single purpose: to serve others. And that purpose is so much greater, so much more meaningful, than anything else.

INDEX

ABOUT THE AUTHOR

For more than 25 years, former CEO and Fortune 500 executive Eric Strafel has dedicated himself to building forward-thinking teams that are empowered to thrive in an increasingly purpose-driven world.

Since founding SUMMi7 in 2019, Eric has focused his efforts on improving business and society by creating opportunities for underrepresented communities. He helps leaders of small and midsize companies learn how to leverage their strengths to grow profits while remaining true to their values and harmonizing all of their pursuits.

Eric was vice president of strategy and market development at Boeing Global Services. Prior to that, he took on leadership of Supplier Management for Boeing Global Services, in addition to his role as CEO of Aviall, where he oversaw record-breaking sales while cultivating frontline leadership. Before joining Aviall, he held positions as vice president of supply chain management at L3 Communications and director of aftermarket spares at Honeywell.

A certified Six Sigma Black Belt, certified Project Management Professional (PMP), and APICS Certified in Production and

Inventory Management (CPIM), Eric sits on the board of directors of the Texas Diversity Council and the Irving Chamber of Commerce.

He has an MBA from Carnegie Mellon University and a bachelor of science in mechanical engineering from Binghamton University. He lives in Texas with his wife and three children.

For more information, visit summi7.com.